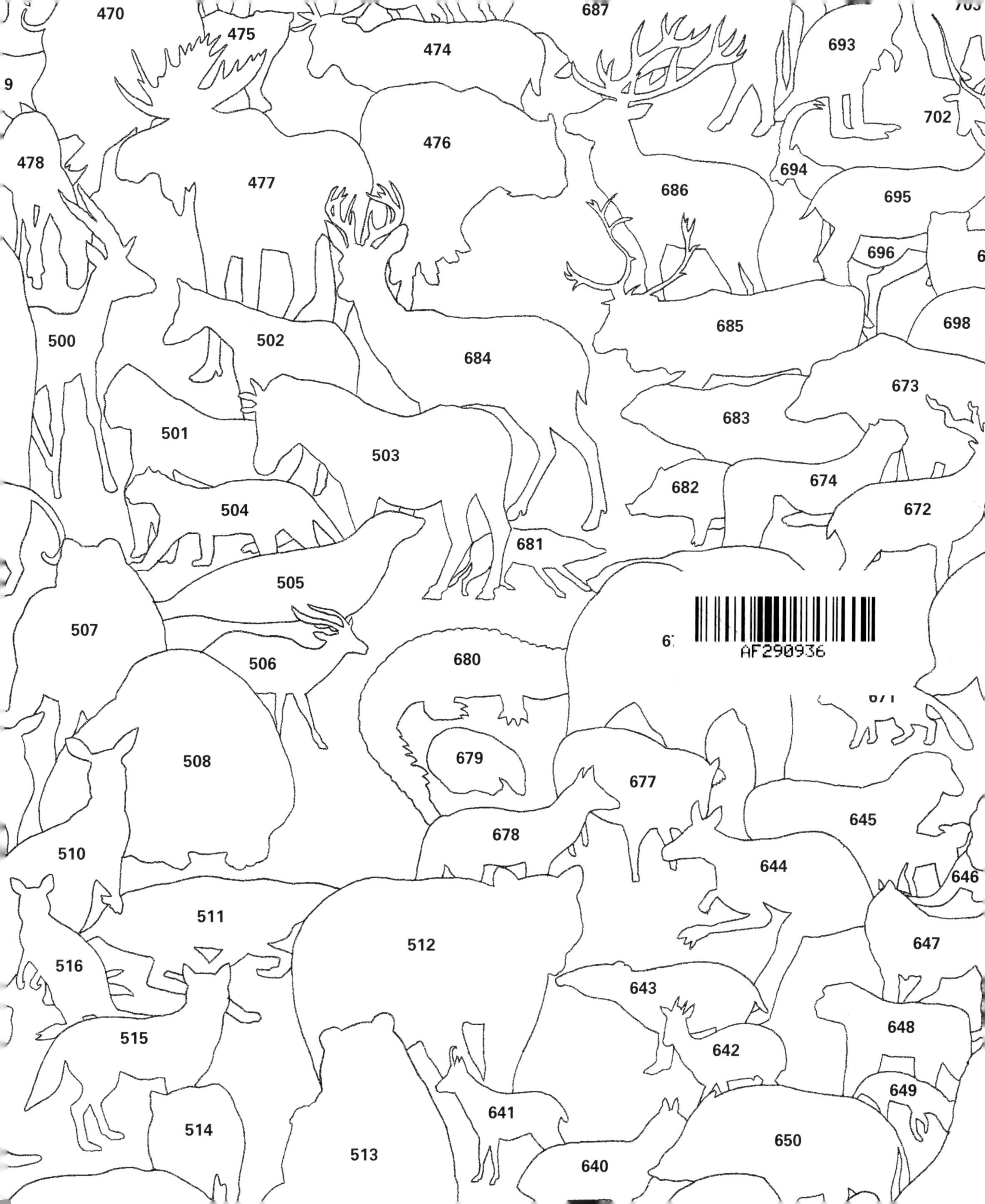

AF290936

Marion Coutts

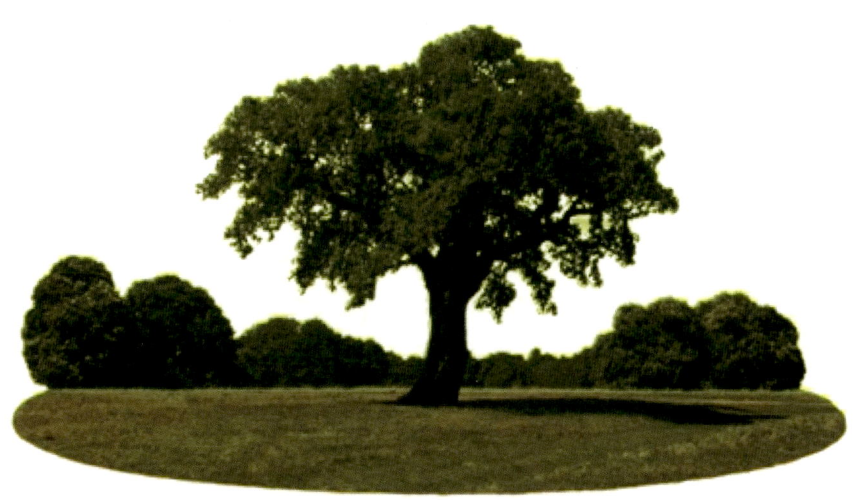

film and video umbrella
firstsite

Marion Coutts' *Everglade* fades up from white like a ghost image materialising on the page. As starkly etched as a scene from a memory, Coutts' haunting landscape cameos (shot in parkland on the outskirts of London) are cropped to resemble the pictorial vignettes used in 18th century engravings; each tracing a different pattern of trees against the absent sky; each capturing the people that we see there in a timeless bubble, or bauble, of light. Standing out from the whiteness of the void that surrounds it, the frame of the vignette makes each image seem hermetic, abstracted, but also lends a strange kind of numinous quality, infusing these everyday scenes with unexpected echoes of an afterlife; each cut-out shape as unique as a snowflake, a receptacle for an individual human soul.

It would be hard to draw an equivalent line round Coutts' body of work as a whole. Subtle, oblique and endlessly inventive, Coutts' art resists easy categorisations, doesn't fit neatly into any overarching frame. This publication (the first substantial overview of her career to date) instead offers a series of pathways through Coutts' vivid and evocative *oeuvre*; some suggested by the three newly commissioned texts, others illuminated by the sheer visual power of Coutts' images themselves.

The book (which focuses mainly on the period 2000–2003, giving roughly equal emphasis to Coutts' object-based and moving-image works) is also part of a wider collaboration between Film and Video Umbrella (the commissioners of *Everglade*) and firstsite, whose survey exhibition of Coutts' work, compiled in association with Angel Row Gallery in Nottingham, includes many of the pieces featured here. I would like to give special thanks to Katherine Wood at firstsite for her contribution to this publication.

Steven Bode
Director, Film and Video Umbrella

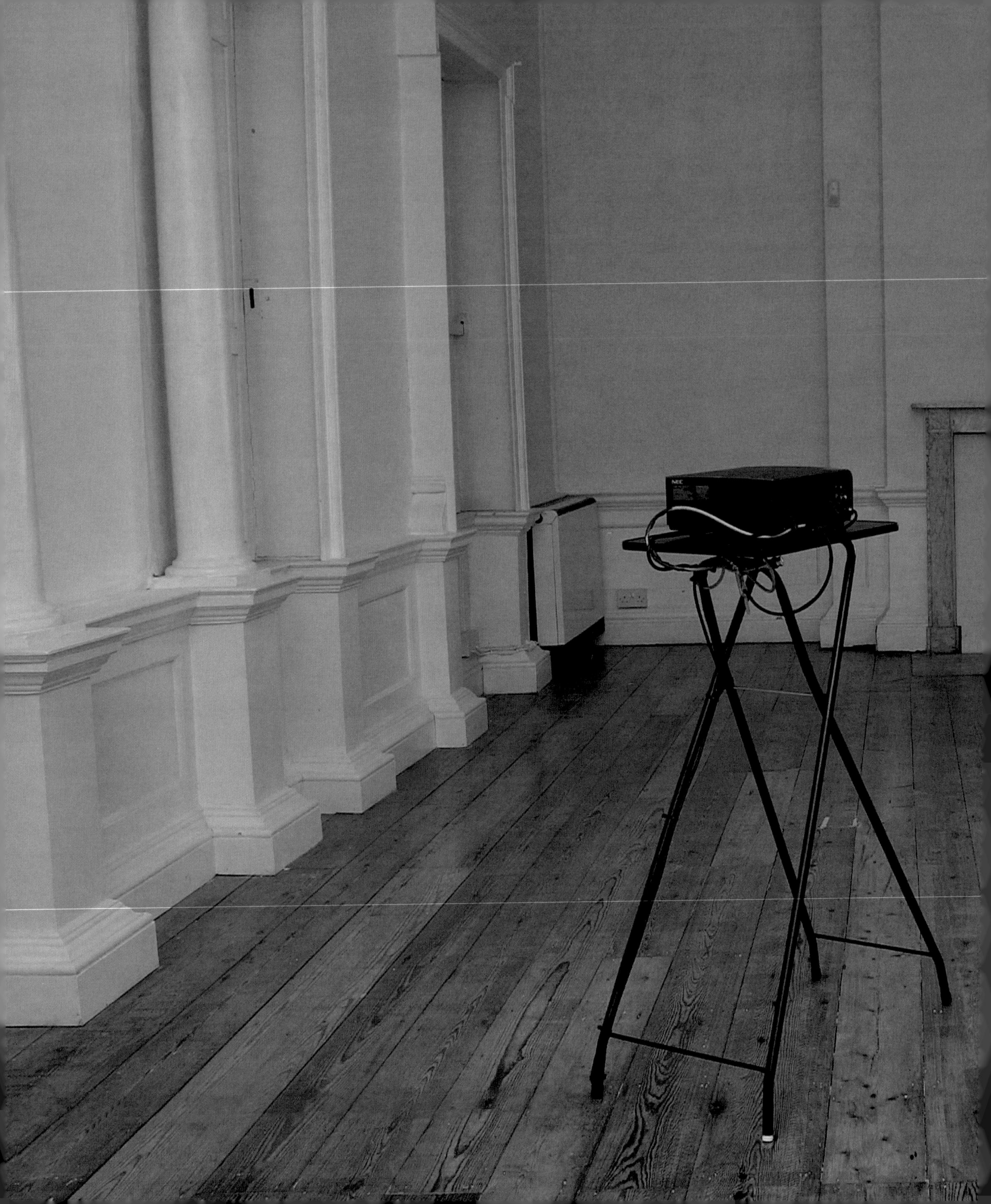

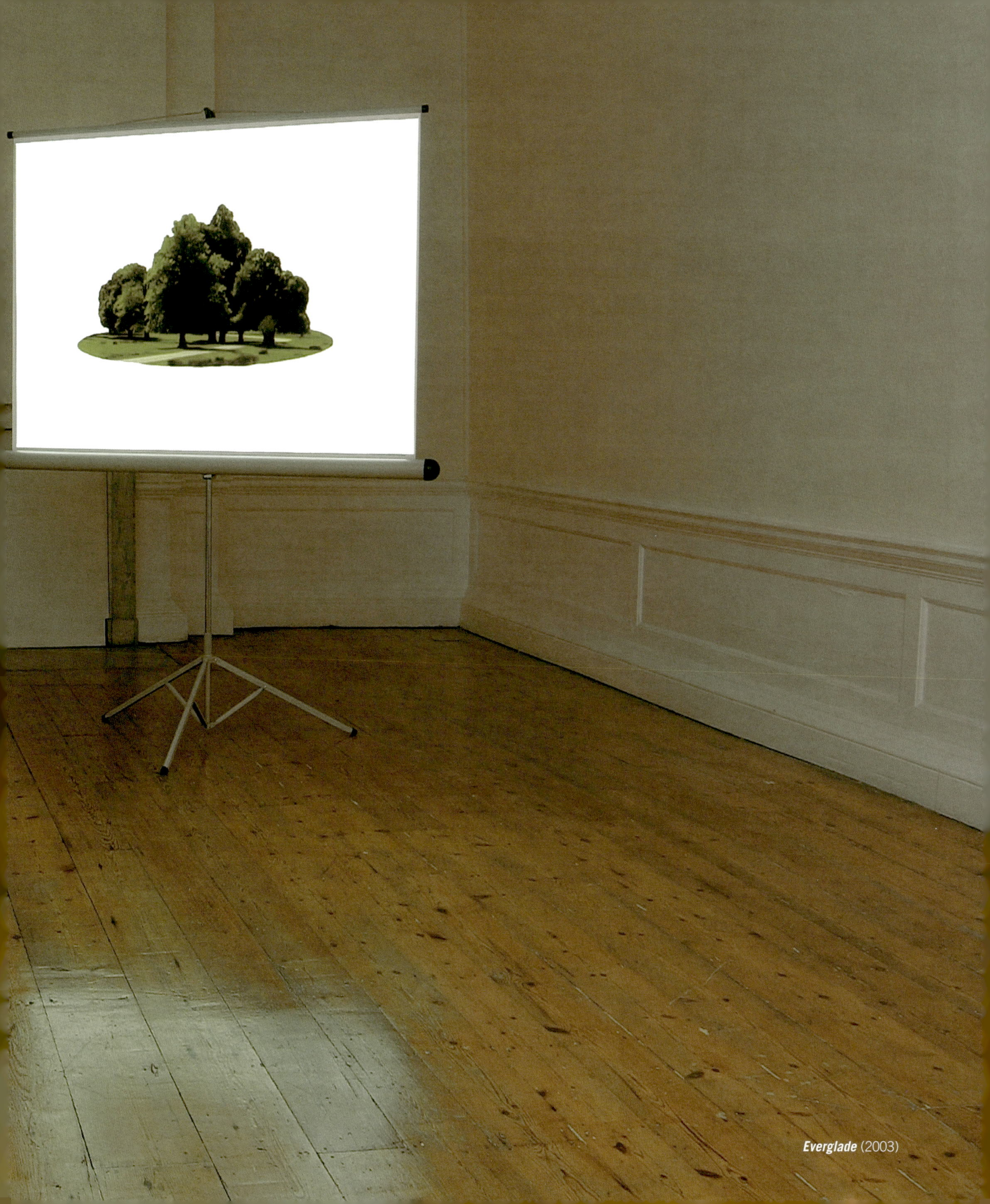

Everglade (2003)

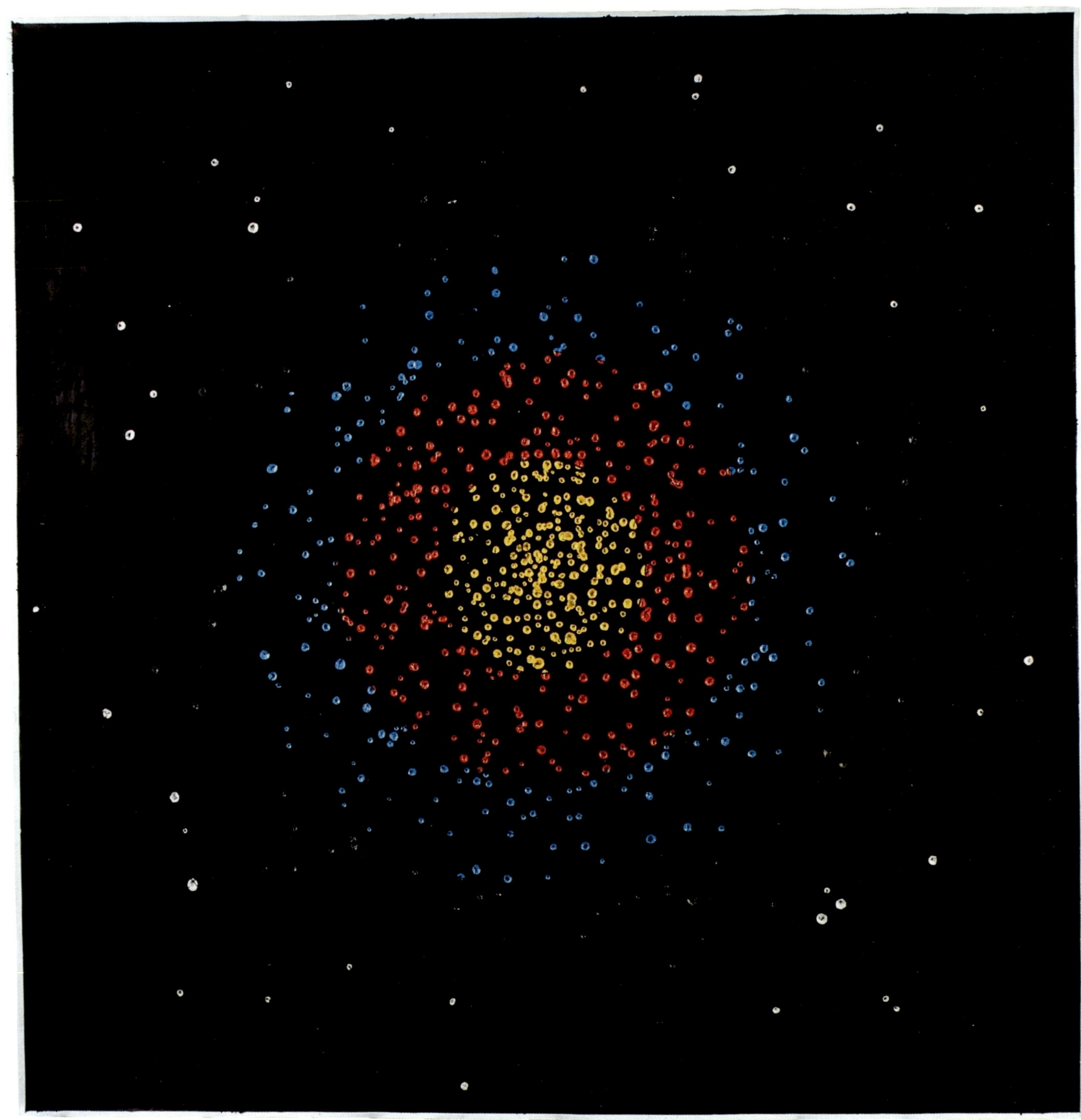

Target Nebula (2003)

Marion Coutts

Sally O'Reilly

A simple, almost vacant act of obliteration is the genesis of Marion Coutts' *Target Nebula*. She has taken a used archery target, its toughened paper perforated all over with arrow-head punctures, and painted it black, leaving just a small perimeter around each piercing. Through the mask of blackness, a stellar cloud of bright and ragged points appears, barely insinuating the concentric coloured rings of the target – yellow, red, blue, black and white – that lurk beneath the layer of paint. More dense toward the centre and dispersing towards the edges, the pattern recalls many mathematical and scientific phenomena, from the big bang to entropy to statistical spreads. The cosmic image suggests questions of creation and design. The configuration of points hints at an elusive kind of purpose. It isn't a random scatter, and it isn't a deliberate plotting. It's more a record of successive failures to achieve a single goal. We might then bring a sociological reading to this abstract idealisation, thinking of conurbation or crowd movement. Or consider the individuals involved, the absent archers who have literally left their mark — the punctures standing for a human group, some club or team, socialising in competition; the aura of impacts around the bull's-eye representing their attempts at perfection, the inconsistent scope of human capability.

Yet to the eye these holes that signify the actions of individuals are completely inter-changeable. They bear no trace of the identity of their makers. They are reduced to the binary status of 'on' or 'hit', a purely statistical value that sheds all connotations of yeomen, savages or Olympians. Physical fact shucks off narrative baggage. The qualitative gives way to the quantitative, sheer number. Despite the process that created it – part unwitting collaboration, part knowing appropriation and interference – the image is autonomous and takes its place among the other blank targets and concen-tricities that have cropped up throughout 20th century art, from Duchamp to Jasper Johns to Richard Long.

Target Nebula is not a typical Coutts piece. There isn't such a thing. Her art as a whole has no single aim, no one guiding thread – a topic, a trick, a look – on which the works can be hung like washing. It goes criss-cross. Between the individual pieces there are many diagonal axes that can be drawn to form an elaborate structure. Effects, motifs or sculptural syntax make communicating doorways that lead from one piece to another within a complex of phenomenological corridors. Formal or thematic links highlight similarities and differences. The lines and the gaps between the works, the echoing discourse amongst them, are as solid as the works themselves. The action of each single piece is condensing, yet expansive. Coutts transforms things so that they send out feelers, gather associations and resound in the world around them. With an investment of humour and complication she tips objects beyond the stability of normal use and meaning, into a dynamic snowball that tumbles and grows in our imagination.

At the same time, each work is a point of intersection in the larger web of works. Each occupies a nodal place in a dense matrix of cross-reference. From *Target Nebula*, for instance, you might take off along various trajectories. You could connect out to Coutts' highly abstract interest in multitudes of elements, masses, regular and irregular formations. Or you could follow Coutts' rich vocabulary of 'social objects', everyday items charged with communal or gathering power: archery targets, table-tennis tables, satellite dishes, funfair lights, gym equipment, lecterns… (they pile up like the contents of an institutional storage cupboard). Or you could keep your eye on the sky.

The wall-sculpture *Some Enchanted Evening* is a wide oblong vista of black velvet 'ring-liners', slotted jeweller's display boards, studded apparently randomly with gold wedding bands. The arrangement of the rings is in fact a representation of the northern sky at night, mapping out the major constellations. The piece presents an image of Romance — star-lit, starry-eyed, horoscopic, a vision of kitsch magic in gold and black velvet, with a soupy soundtrack from 'South Pacific'. It is also something more severe. As the London Underground tube map is a schematic version of the real undulations of the train tracks, Coutts' constellations are similarly rigid, constrained by the grid of slots in the display, filled or empty. The piece is constructed again from a binary pattern of 'on' and 'off'. The rings denote 'on' or 'twinkle' in the relevant position, while the vacant slots not only refer to 'no star', or deep space, but also to a ring that has been bought, a romance that has already been initiated, a splice made, that is now flourishing or fizzling out somewhere. Absence, so often used to imply deficit or sadness, here raises a question mark, a lateral proposal of possibilities.

Until his recent death, John the Jeweller of Milford Manufacturers, Auckland, New

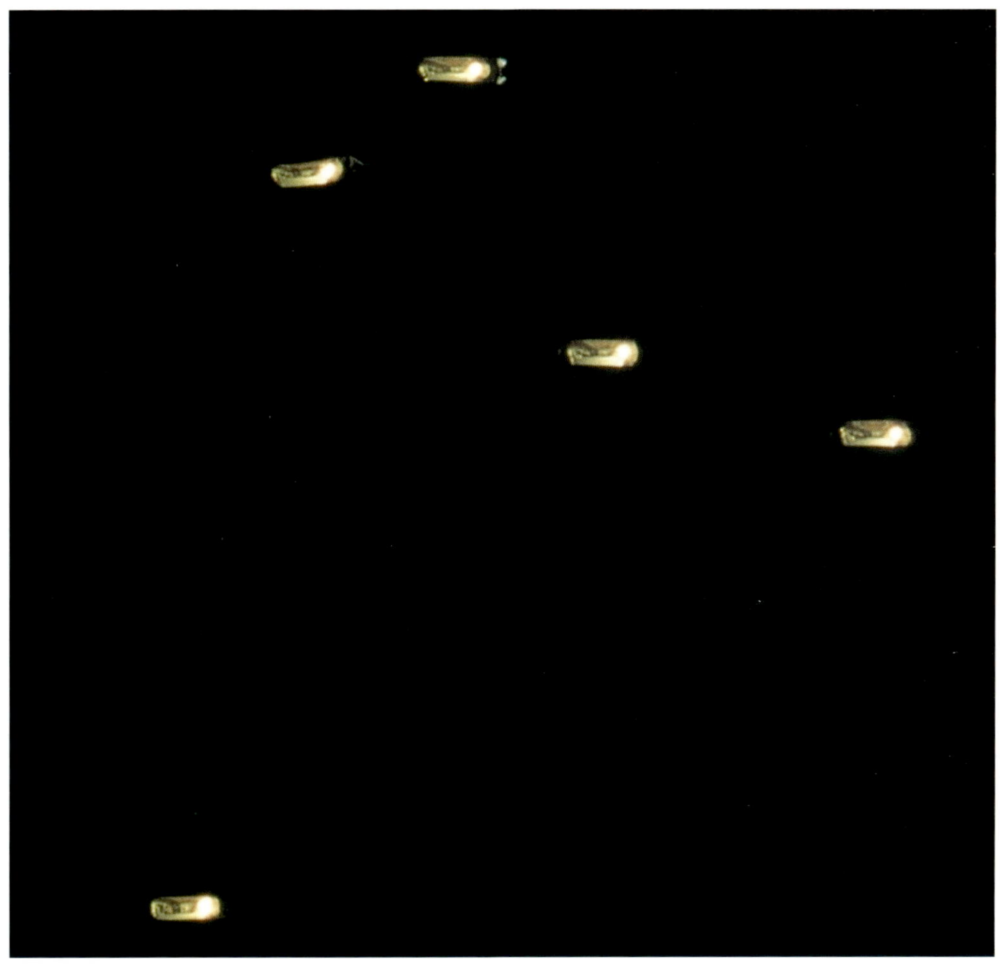

detail from Some Enchanted Evening (2001)

Zealand, manufactured stick pins in the shape of Kiwi birds for American Mormon missionaries. The brooches would have little indentations made around the perimeter of the shape so that the brothers could insert a diamanté for each soul acquired — a digital opposite of Coutts' notation for souls yet to be coupled off. These units of emotion – diamantés and rings – are identical, mere points on a grid that can be reduced to faceless numbers. *Some Enchanted Evening* looks both ways: up at the stars and down on human affairs. It accentuates the apparent contradiction between individual hopes and the remote, statistical overview. Celestial pattern re-orients as social survey.

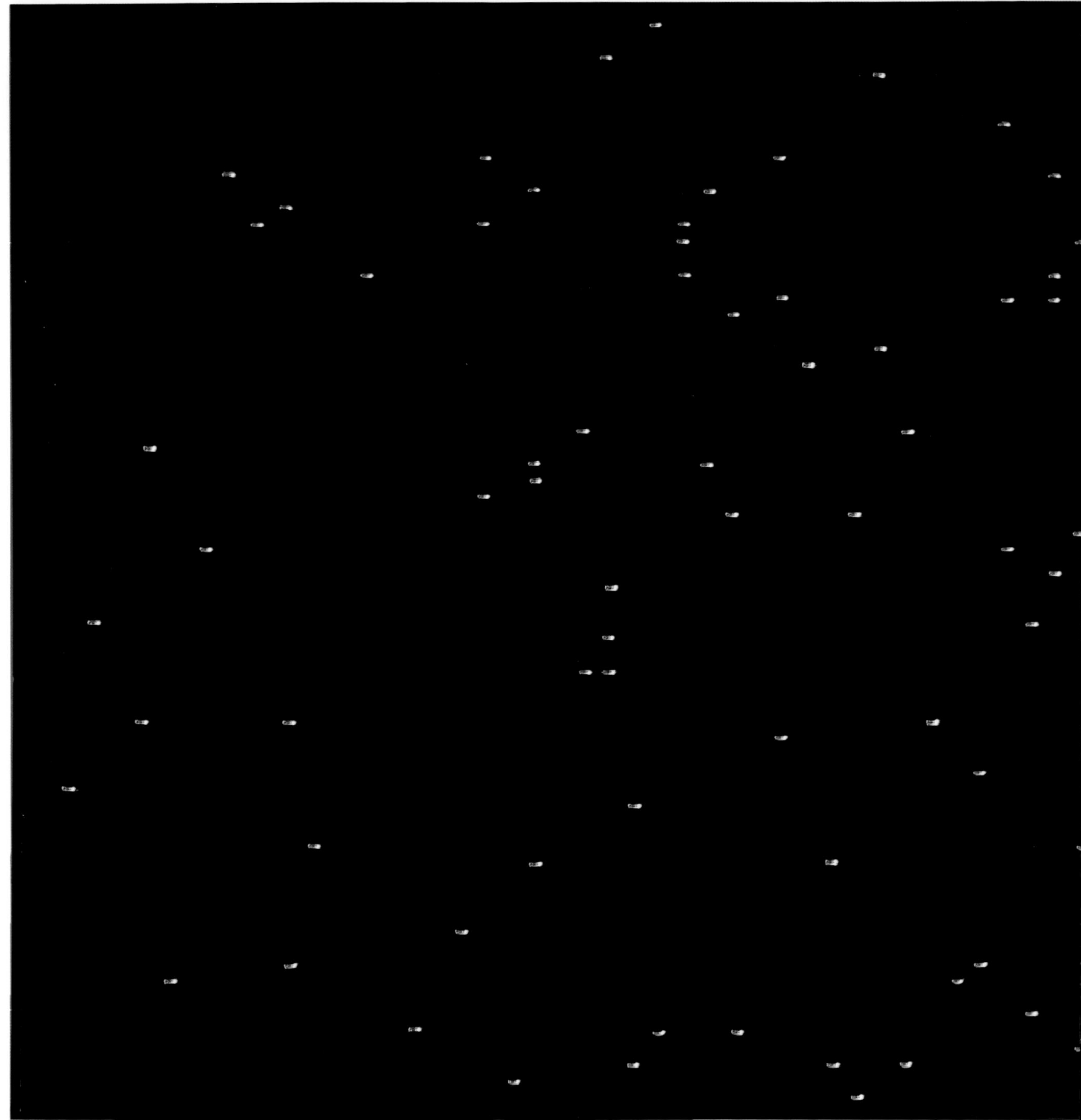

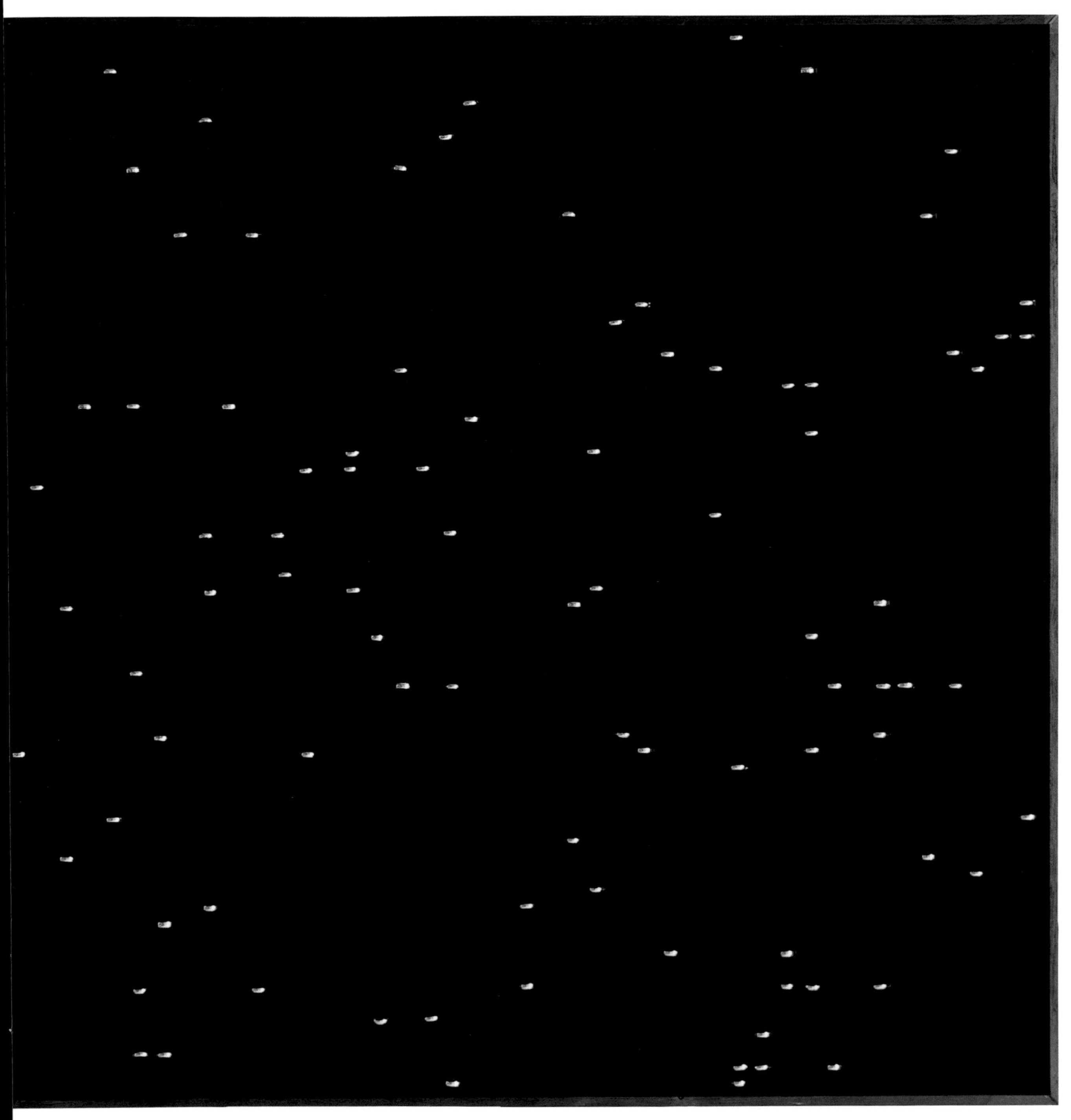

Some Enchanted Evening (2001)

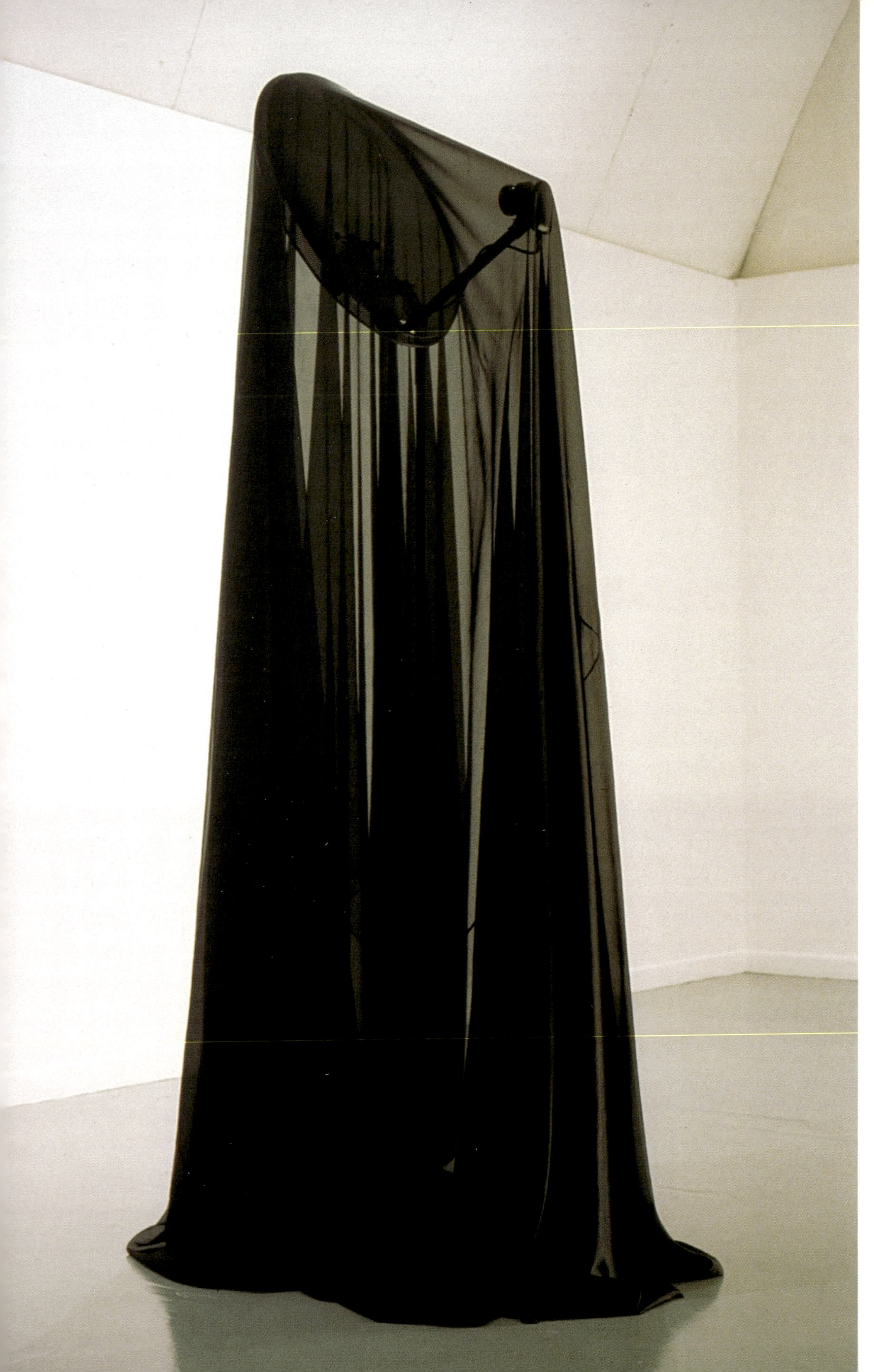

Sibyl (2001)

A mechanical-spiritual bride, *Sibyl* stands eight feet tall, a satellite dish raised on a pole and draped to the floor in black voile. The perforated see-through dish is materially echoed in the finer mesh of the gauze. The cascading folds of translucent fabric obscure the pole so that the upturned face of the dish and its proboscis appear to be spectrally floating — a medium, levitating, pointing skywards. The title evokes the women of the ancient Mediterranean world believed to be inspired oracles or prophetesses (depicted in the floor mosaics in Siena Cathedral and Michelangelo's Sistine Chapel ceiling). Beneath its shroud, the all-too-knowable satellite dish, standing for the trashier side of contemporary culture, becomes a grave mythical enigma capable of communication with the divine. But *Sibyl* could also be thought of as an arc or a fold in time, uniting the popular cultures of two distant eras.

Target Nebula, *Some Enchanted Evening*, *Sibyl*: in these three works, Coutts' play of cross-connections (thematic and formal) is already in action: the covering sky, the concealing/revealing mask, the digital/binary character, the individual and the collective, communal leisure. Each piece picks up on the others, points the way to others still.

With his notion on *différance*, Jacques Derrida proposes that "every concept is inscribed in a chain or in a system within which it refers to the other, to other concepts, by means of the systematic play of differences." An object or sign is determined by the dynamism between what it is, what it is close to and what is completely different to it. Wittgenstein's *family resemblance* offers another sense of how things assemble. "We see a complicated network of similarities overlapping and criss-crossing: sometimes overall similarities, sometimes similarities of detail... the various resemblances between members of a family: build, features, colour of eyes, gait, temperament, etc. etc. overlap and criss-cross in the same way."

Coutts' work happens somewhere between these two models, between an open-ended relay of difference, and the more contained ties of a family gathering. As such, it engages some fundamental questions (questions with aesthetic, philosophical, cognitive, social, biological, religious dimensions): what is it that constitutes a group, a pattern, a connected sequence, an overall plan? This is enacted in the shape of her developing *oeuvre*. At any point in its history it holds together tightly through its multiple connections — but with nothing to tell how or where it might next extend itself and re-assemble. It appears also in the work's array of related concerns, its interest in formations, collectives, mass

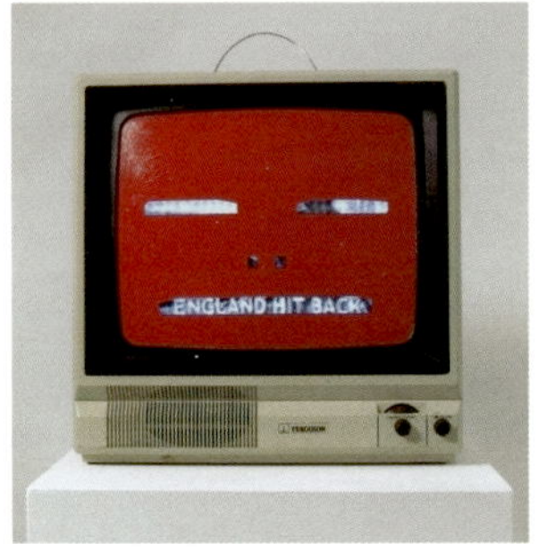

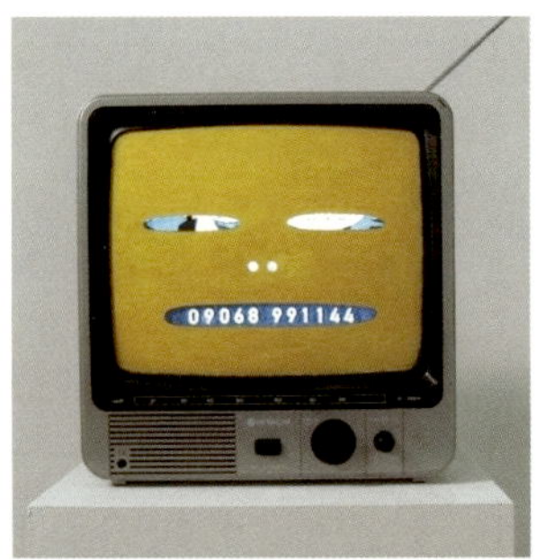

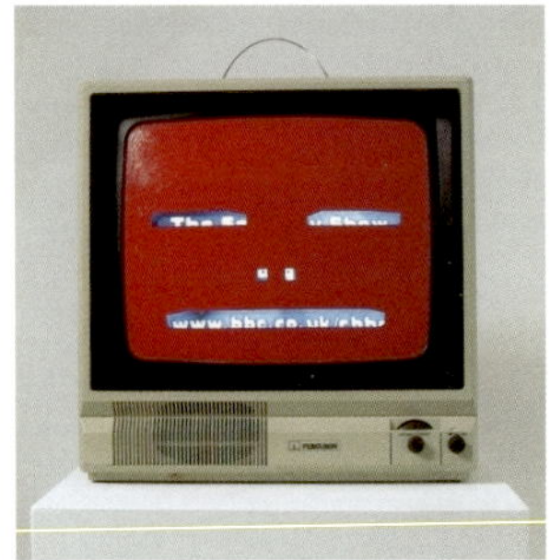

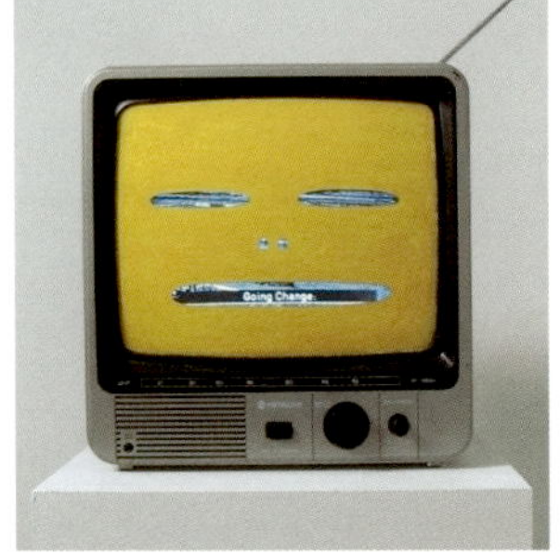

movements, communal behaviour, in the operation – at the most formal and the most human level – of centripetal forces.

There is that supremely centripetal object, the TV: gathering signals from the ether, attracting a mass audience, a nucleus for domestic get-togethers or a companion for the solitary. *The Expressionists* are two portable black-and-white television sets with Halloween pumpkin faces painted on their screens in bright colours, gurning like Cartman from 'South Park'. The sets are on, tuned to different stations, broadcasting whatever is being broadcast, the sound down. The flickering images, made up of phosphorescent dots, can only be seen through their eyes, nose and mouth holes so that there are prime moments of happenstance when subtitles appear in the mouth, or a celebrity looks out from one of the eyes. *The Expressionists* seem out of control of their feelings as they react alchemically to their internal weather. The TV is its own viewer. The painted faces absorb the content of the programme or advert running behind them, emoting with the transmission, turning the banalities of daytime television into something totemic or jolly. The vintage of the televisions – like many of Coutts' objects, they look well-used – gives them a benevolent familiarity so that they can't be mistaken for austere gallery monitors; they are end-of-the-bed or kitchen counter tellies, intimate household friends that, like *Sibyl*, bring messages from the world beyond our walls.

The Expressionists, with their TV heads, are an immediate precursor to the large video installation, *Cult*. In a wide low-lit gallery, nine small monitors, on plinths that raise them to the average viewer's sight-line, play a video of the same cat's face as it gazes at the camera, occasionally closing its eyes. The video has been re-edited for each monitor, so that every cat contributes to a slow-paced fugue of blinks and stares. This cult animal, object of both ancient and contemporary devotion, is made into a cultic group, gathered in a ritual vigil, that raises anxieties of exclusion and alienation. As the viewer walks around the darkened space, through the copse of monitors, there is an uncomfortable feeling that the cabal of cats are communicating with one another, a feeling made all the more uncanny by the fact that it is the same cat on each monitor. The effect is of a preternatural power, a disquieting multiplicity — a realignment of the power structure between the domestic pet and adoring owner.

Animal life is another thread in Coutts' web. *Cult* is one of a series of video works where animals appear; part allegorical signifiers, part behavioural specimens. In *Break*, three

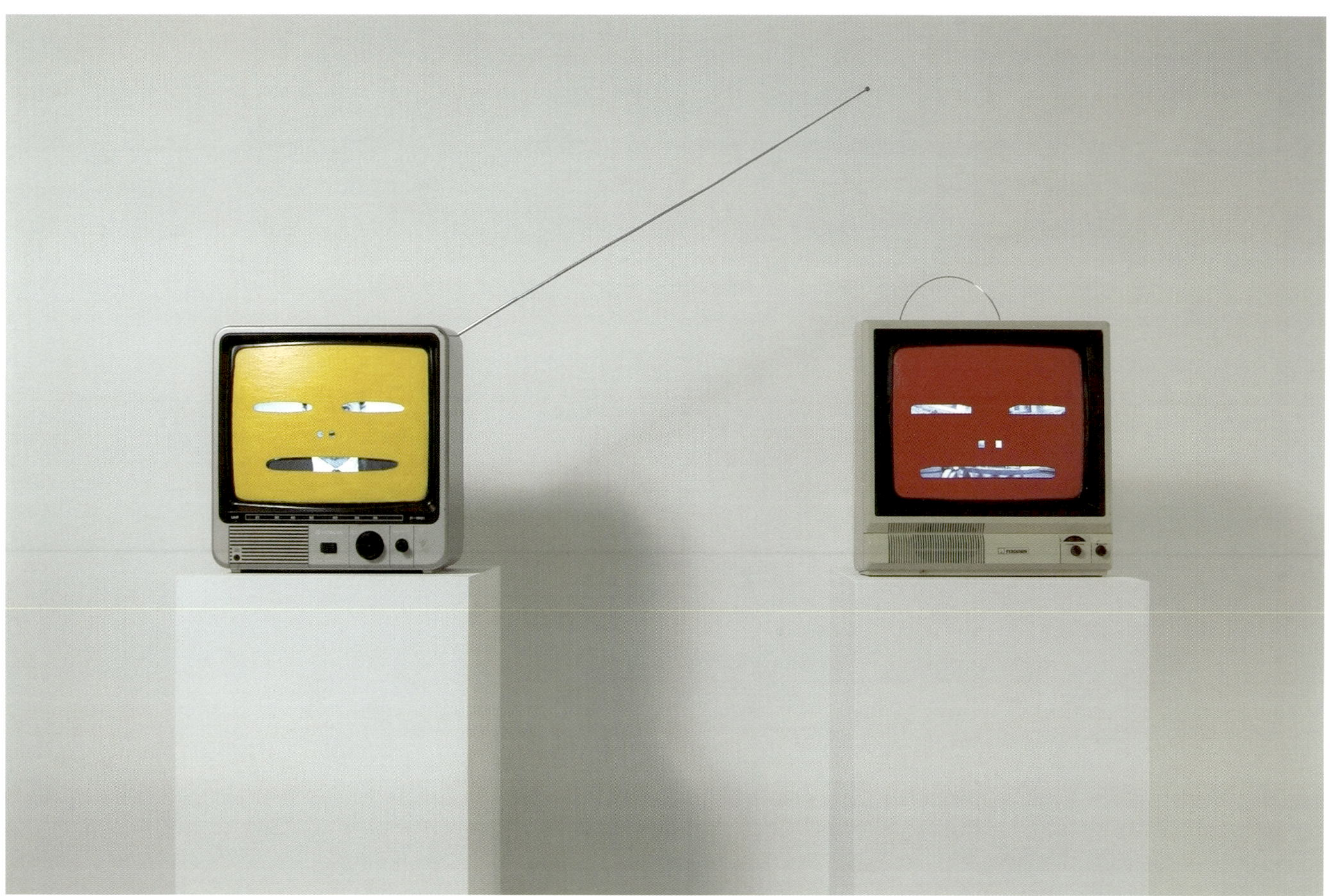

The Expressionists (2001)

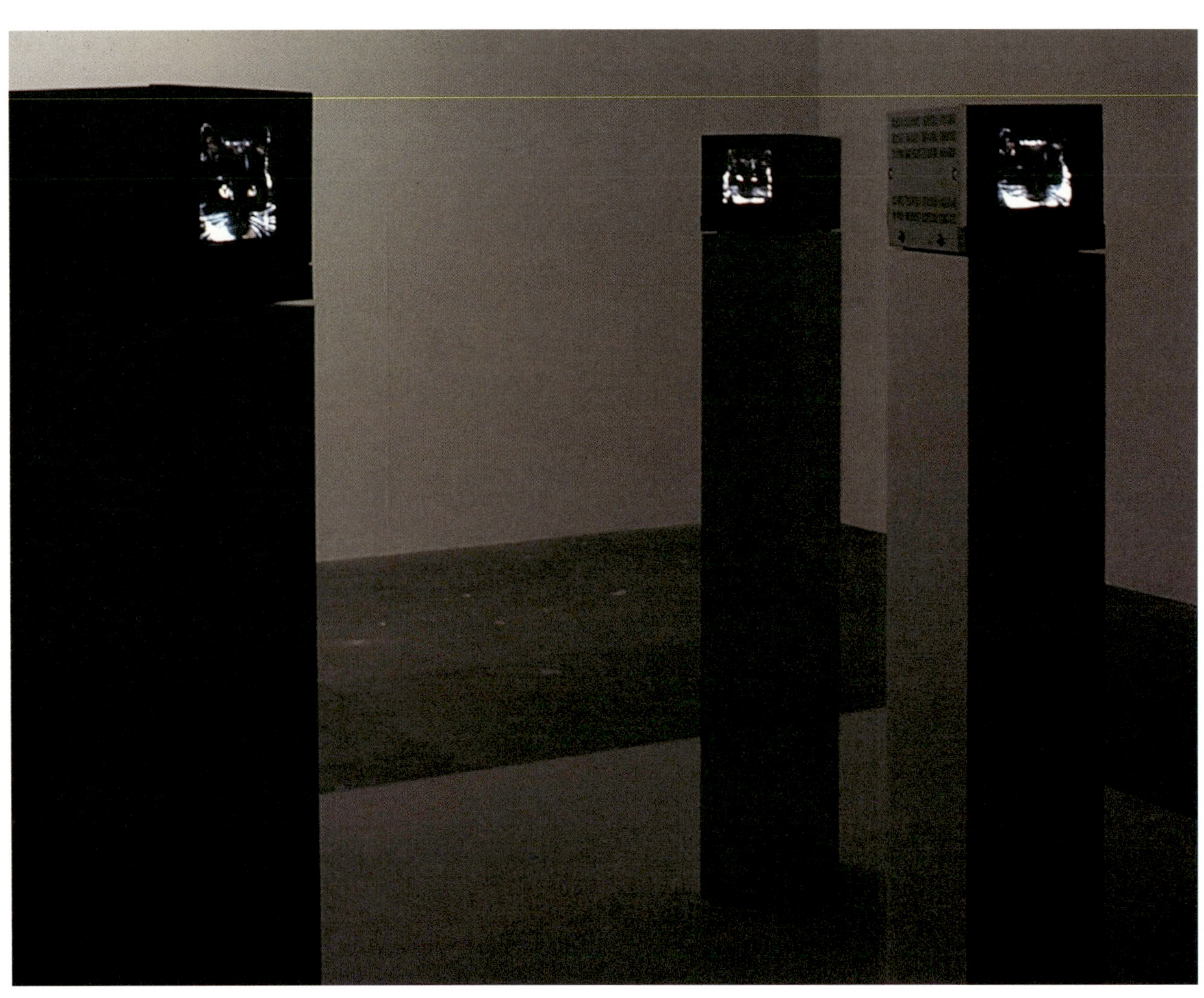

Cult (2002) – installation at Chisenhale Gallery

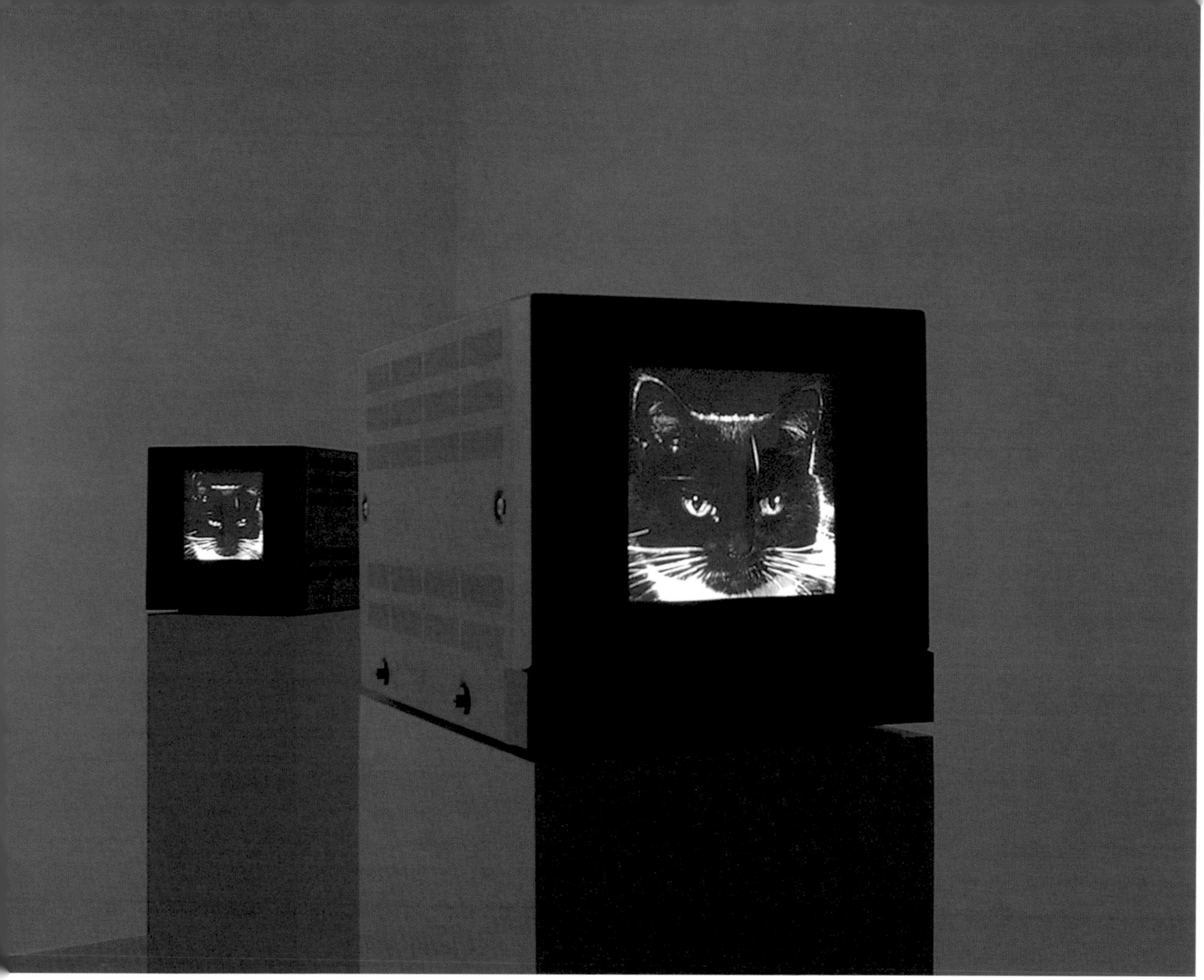

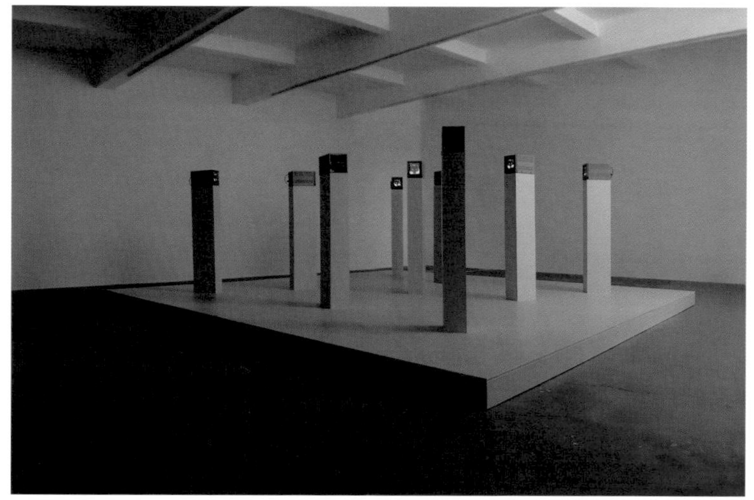

hamsters in exercise balls ricochet around a confined run. In *No Evil Star*, a seething mass of mealworms dominates a model landscape. These are both straight projection pieces. *Assembly* is a symbiosis of video and found object. A wooden lectern stands before you, its tilted 'rest' making a screen for a continuous projection showing flocking starlings, as they swoop, dissipate and regroup in an open sky. The lectern is both literal and contextual support. The educational or ecclesiastical associations of the object rub off on the video imagery, so that overtones of mass control, determinism and institutionalised actions become intertwined with the natural spectacle. There is also a literary or polemic aura to the piece: the birds' flight, with its change of direction, density and pace, could be transcribed into the narrative flow of a biblical tract, political speech or academic lesson.

This synaesthetic transfer between media, disciplines or sensibilities is a fundamental procedure in Coutts' work. Objects are pushed to their extremes, extending their identity into multi-layered agglomerations of reference, elaborations of the joke: when is a door not a door?

A scarred and battered vaulting horse is inscribed with the war memorial epitaph FOR THE FALLEN. It becomes simultaneously a cenotaph, a barrier, a support, a minimal, geometric solid, a personal memory jogger. Most of us have some memory of a vaulting horse: either that of dread, direct from school days, or secondary experience from film, most prominently its appearance as central alibi in the POW escape movie 'The Wooden Horse' (1950). Coutts' *For the Fallen* hyphenates war and sport and school, and recalls their respective casualties. A direct relative of *Assembly*, it carries connotations of institutional discipline and unconditional compliance with counter-intuitive commands. It is not generally in the individual's interest to risk their neck jumping over large objects, but mostly we fall into line.

The opposition of individual and collective furnishes the study of history, sociology, ethics etc, with a vast area of discussion. Different political models, from liberal democracy to dictatorship, place different expectations on the individual within society. In popular culture, too, stories of utopias, dystopias, failure, ambition, heroes and zombies focus on this relation of one to many. War movies, for instance, dramatise the individual's visibility by elevating the hero to the camera's lens above thousands of others who are shown as acting *en masse* – especially if they are the enemy.

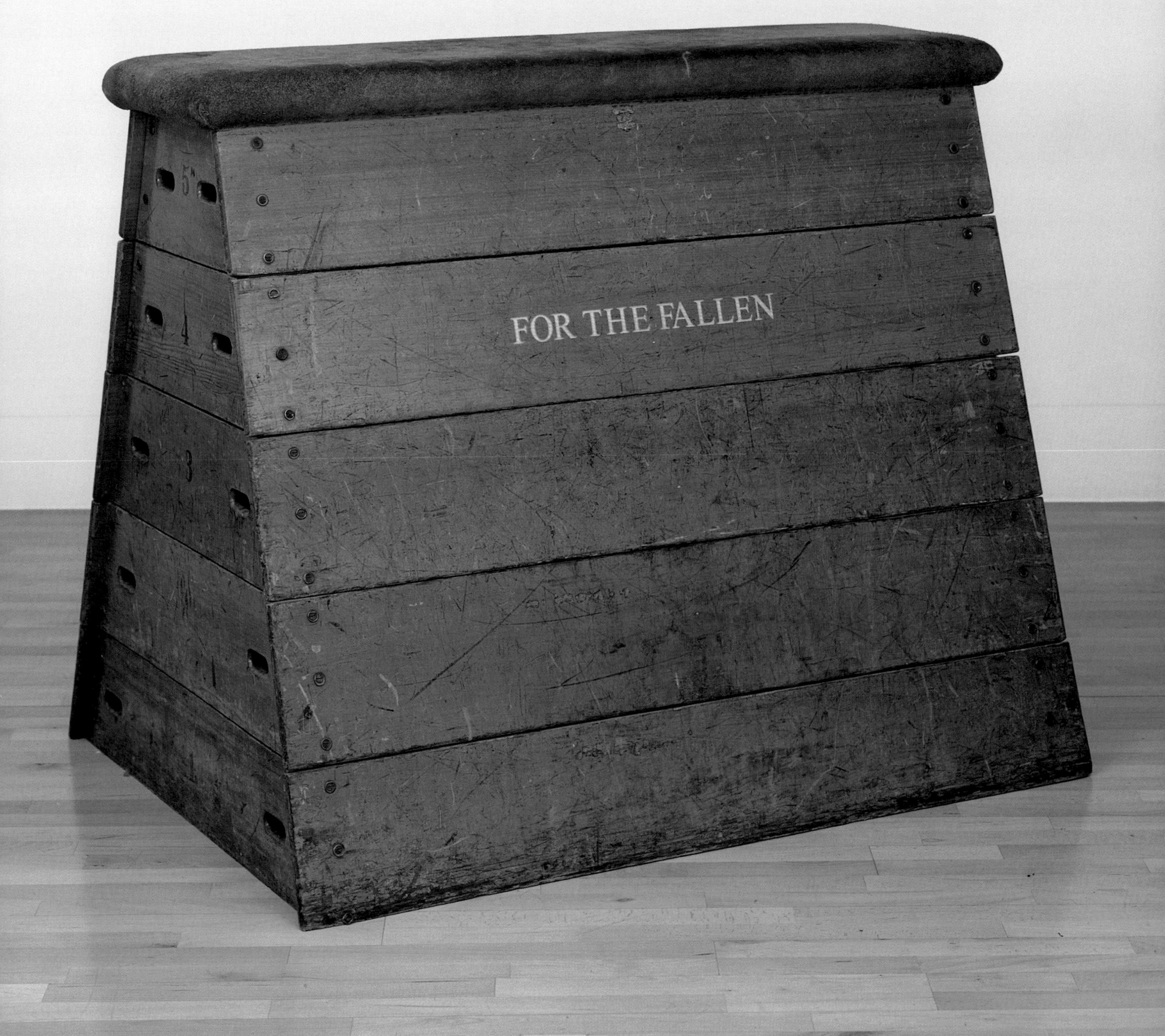

5"
4
3
FOR THE FALLEN

In his essay 'The Genesis of the Individual' (1992), the French philosopher of science Gilbert Simondon proposes a post-humanist model that does not tolerate an inner, objective essence, and in which the organic and inorganic are no longer distinguished from one another. The emphasis is placed on systems of actions, so that an individual or object is a 'metastable equilibrium', defined by its effect on and differences from the world, by the shape it makes and the shape the world makes around it. Simondon outlines a reciprocal, self-informing feedback loop that existence in a society implies. Coutts' hybridising actions, her interstitial creations, illustrate this reflexivity and interdependency. The identity of each object lies neither in its appearance nor its function, but in its unfolding relationship with its fellow works, with our experience and expectations.

The floor-sculpture, *Money*, is itself a fluid play of individuation, of organic and inorganic. Masses of pennies (another twinkling multitude) are scattered in dense slurries around the gallery. Money, a confusion of sign and object, a physical embodiment of an ideal, abstract meaning, is the ultimate 'social object'. Whether we find it embarrassing, desirable, elusive, beautiful or ugly, money has an almost unique potency and allure. When money shows its face – coins dropped on the pavement, cascading in arcade machines, gathering in buskers' instrument cases, languishing underwater in fountains and wishing wells – the sight grabs the eye.

But in *Money* it becomes a formless mass of stuff, a protozoic organism. Thousands of copper bits, their shiny metal reflecting the light to create an illusion of wetness, coalesce into a flux, out of which arise in turn small but solid mounds, little piles of money, breasts or pats, which seem to swim around, and then fuse together or split apart, reproducing like amoebas. Money breeds, adds up, divides, multiplies. The metaphors are simultaneously sexual and mathematical. Money is at its business. A normally ordered substance, dictated by the logic of counting, has been released into a state of ambiguity and contained chaos.

Base collective matter appears here at its most sticky. But Coutts' work has its moments of transcendence too — in its visions of open spaces, in the skies of *Assembly* and the deep night of *Some Enchanted Evening*. Open space, as a site for release and escape, is difficult to iterate in an image or object on a domestic or gallery scale. Distance, infinity must be suggested in precarious and lateral ways. *Some Enchanted*

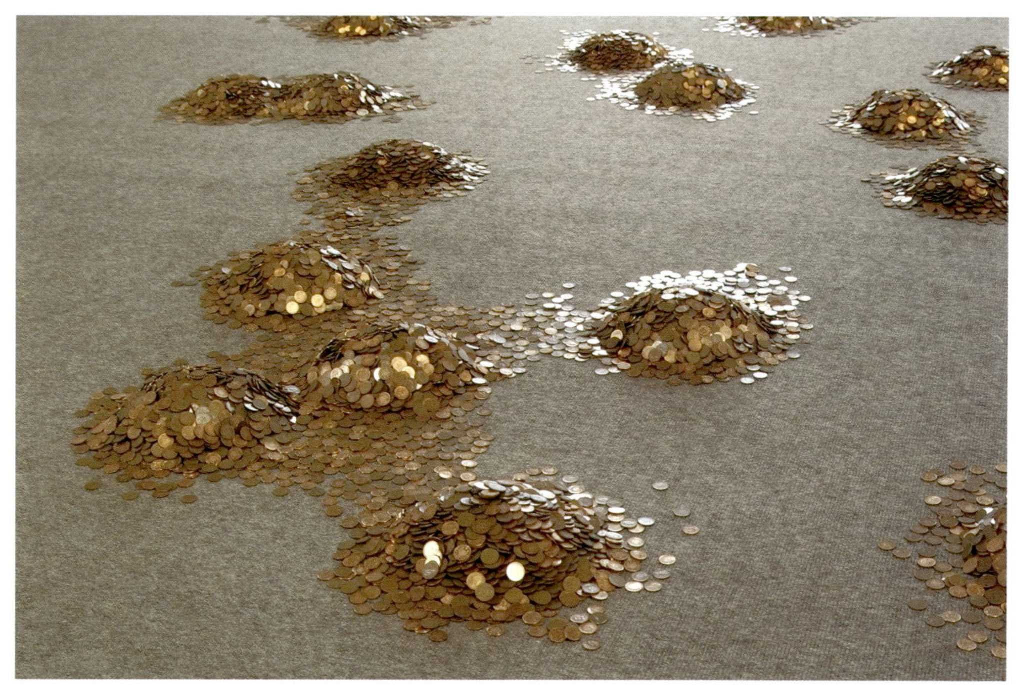

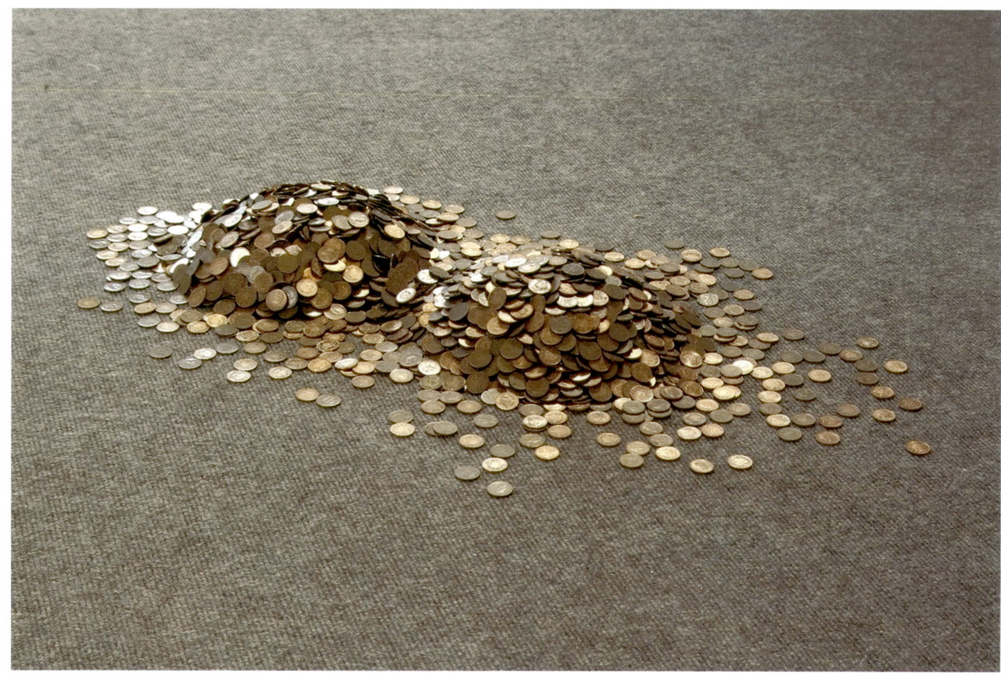

details from **Money** (2003)

Evening expands by implying possibility through absence. *Assembly*, fitting a small section of sky precisely onto a lectern top, hints at infinity by its artificial boundary. The video installation *Everglade* also intimates potential through containment.

The piece uses a standard home movie set up: projector on stand, screen on tripod, moving image. Video footage shows sunny, leafy parks, like a memory of a nice day out. The pictures, though, have been trimmed into vignettes. The normal rectangular format of the image is cropped and condensed, turning segments of park into islands of landscape in the middle of the white screen, fragile think bubbles, floating in a vacuum of light. Occasionally, people walk through these sub-urban idylls. But *Everglade* is above all a meditation on a subtle narrative of landscape: each image only barely visibly a moving image, still but for the breeze in the grass and trees; each scene alternately vacant and briefly inhabited, and between times dissolving entirely into light. Light is the agent that carries the image towards the screen, where it is held hovering like a mirage within its white surround, intermittently vanishing, the mental picture blanking. *Everglade* stages an endless, dreamy, melancholy dialogue between leisure, landscape and void.

Viewpoints switch, perspectives swoop. In Marion Coutts' work we shift between the widest angle and the narrowest focus, between mass and unit, mythic and mundane, objective overview and subjective experience, from the most remote and abstract configuration of elements to the most particular objects. And in these shifts, these soundings across distance, in the patterns of connection and the gaps that remain, the work seems to grasp something — a field of knowledge, a body of feeling; a revelation, briefly glimpsed, of the whole thing, of how it all comes together.

Money (2003)

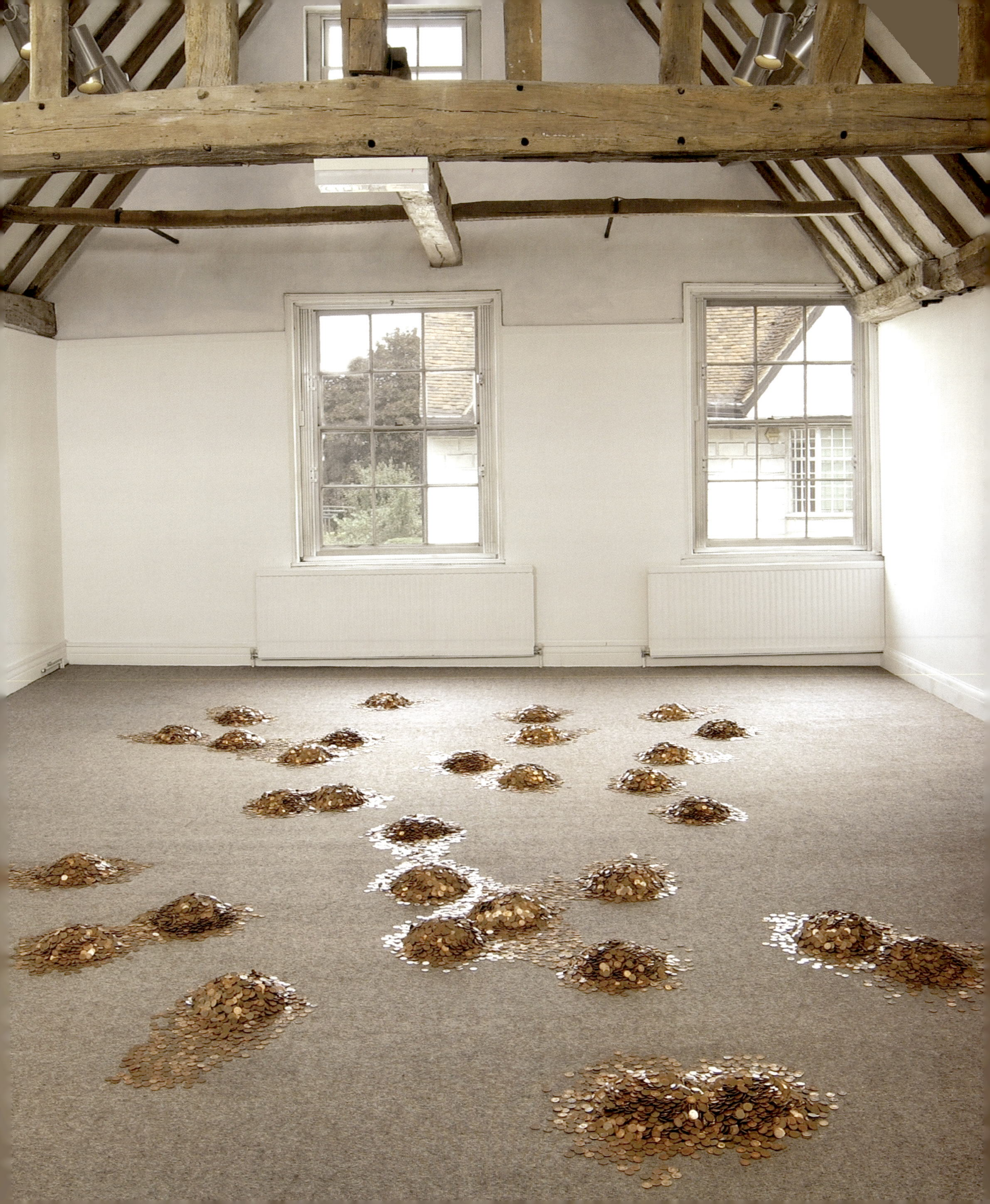

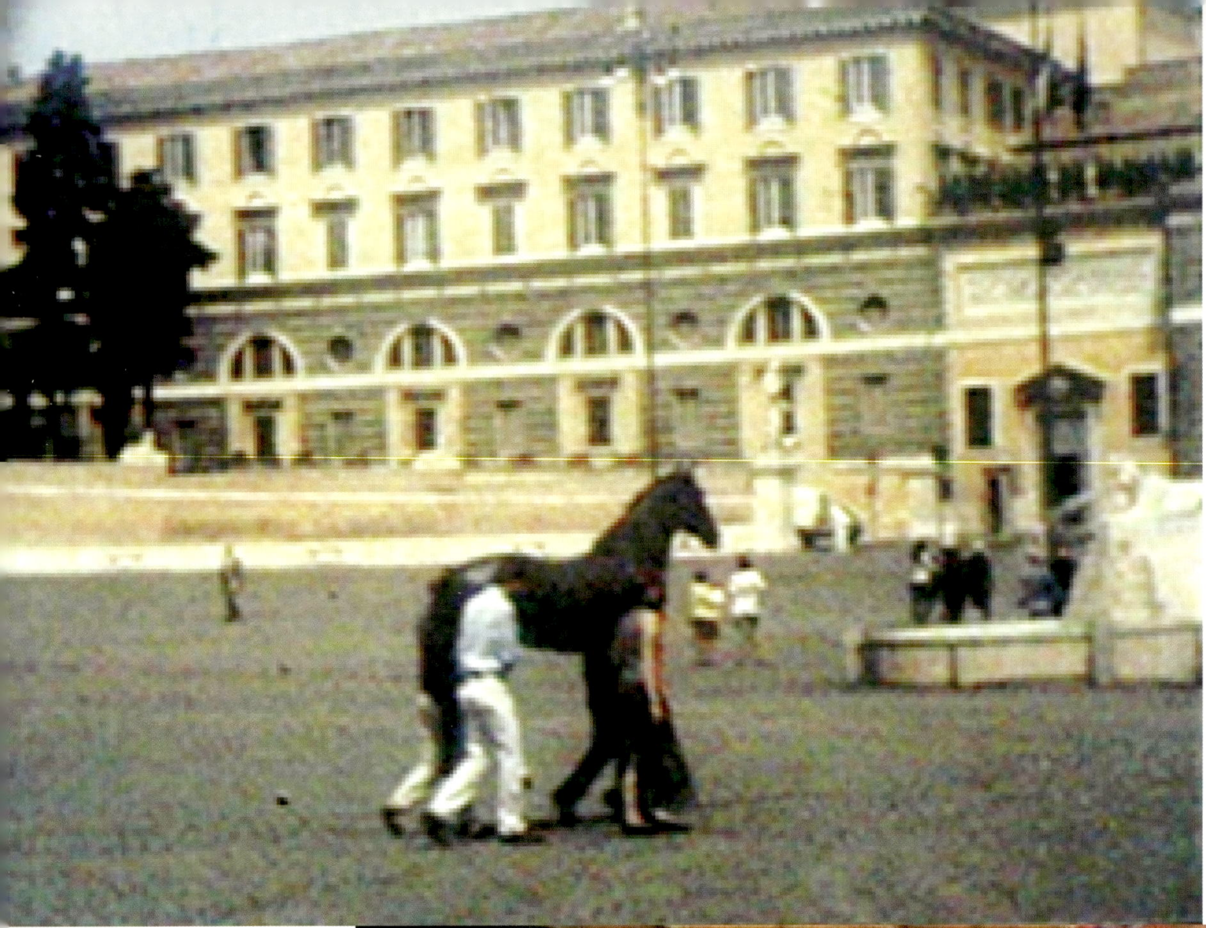

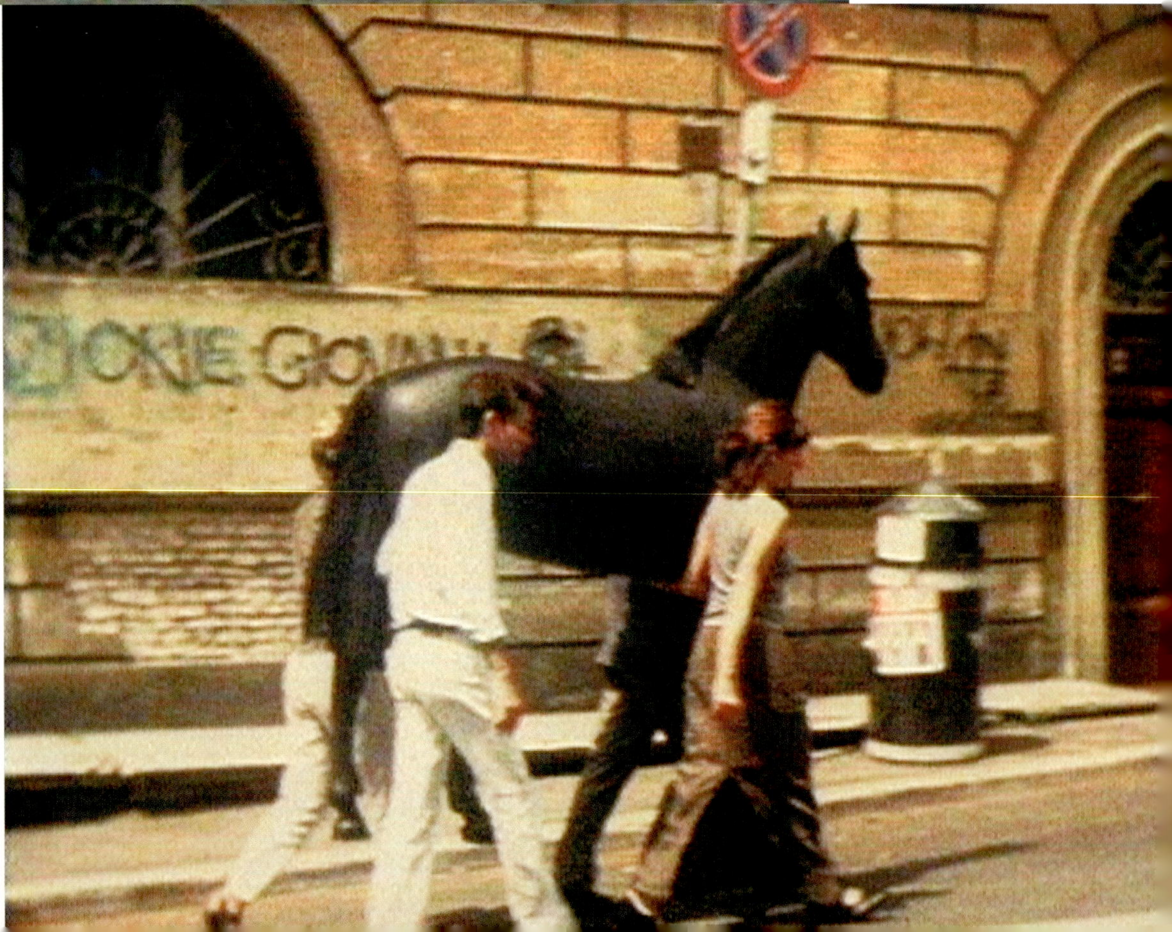

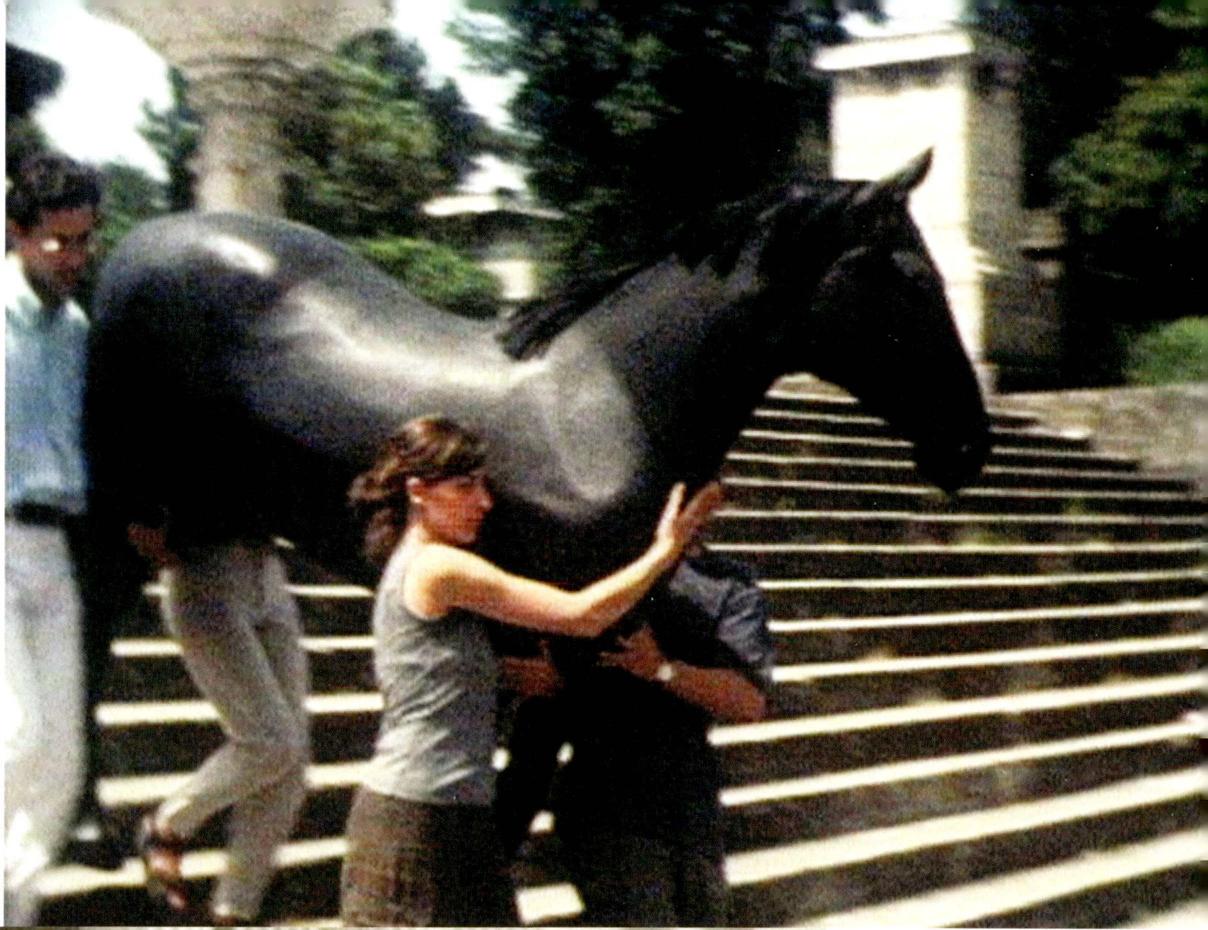

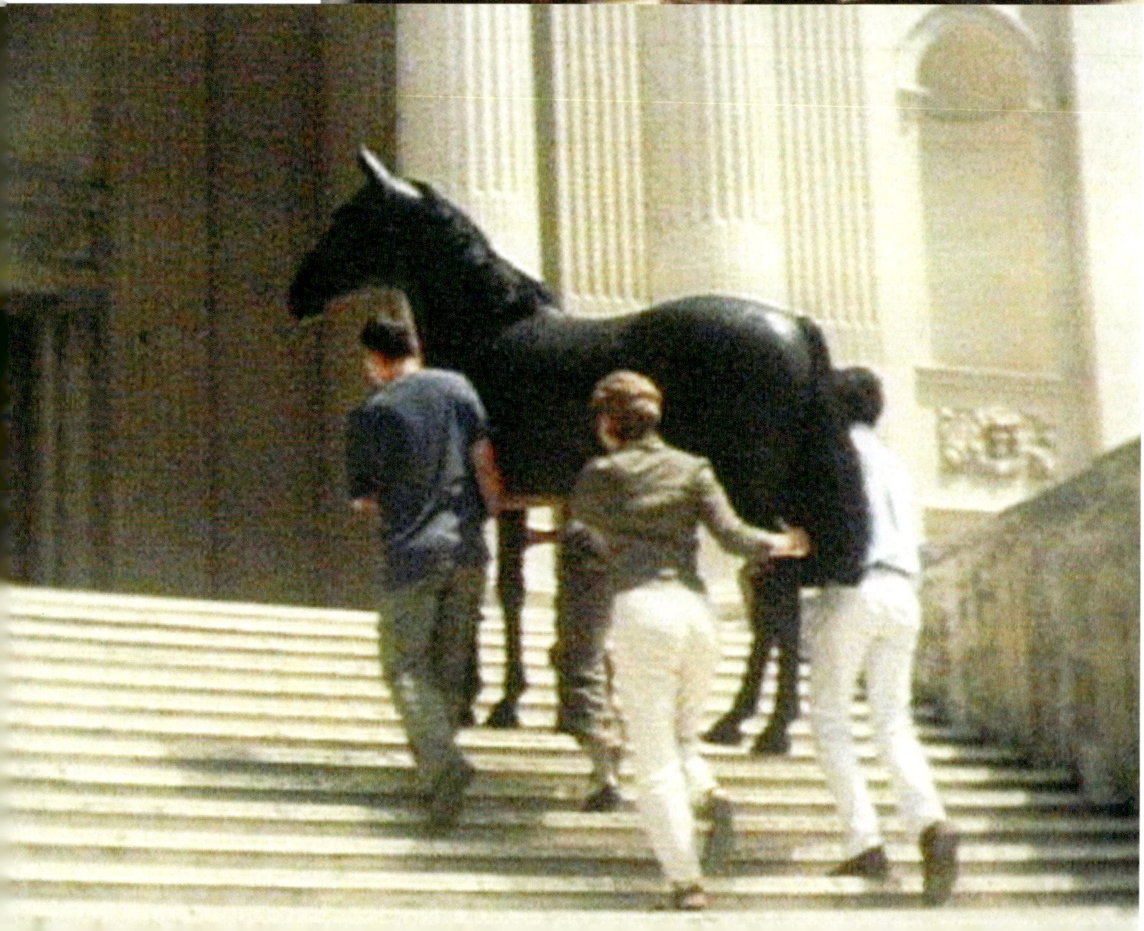

epic (2000)

Everglade

Marion Coutts in conversation with Katherine Wood

Katherine Wood: Titles and naming are important in your practice. Why *Everglade*?
Marion Coutts: My aunt had a boarding house for the elderly in Worthing. It was called 'The Haven'. I always thought 'Everglade' would be a good name for a home of rest or a retirement village. These places often try and blur the difference between life and life-after-death. Idealised images of retirement are very like concepts of the afterlife and Heaven — eternal leisure, eternal stasis, wandering through green parkland. So, though the work doesn't refer to retirement as such, the title connects with those dream-like images of perpetual leisure.

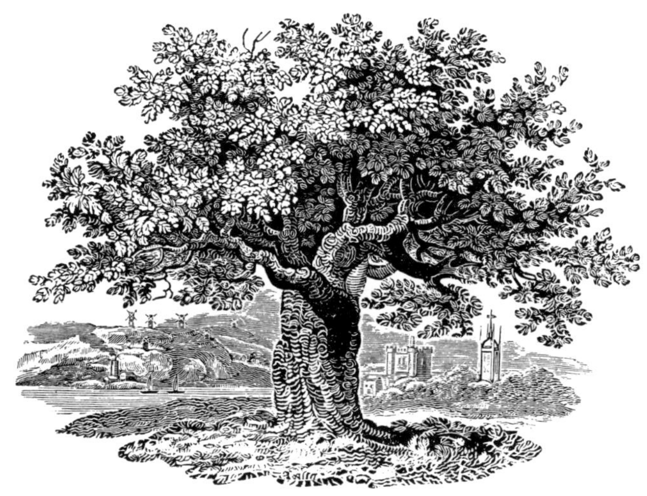

The imagery has a strong element of the visionary or utopian.
I had been thinking about visionary images, in part remembered from illustrations in evangelical tracts, like the 'Paradise' of the Jehovah's Witnesses, always crowded with fruit, animals and the Saved. I was brought up in the Salvation Army; not as a body very interested in images, but with its illustrated magazines 'The Young Soldier' and 'The War Cry', and where the action of dying is known as 'Promotion to Glory'. I was

Woodcut by Thomas Bewick (*c.* 1800)

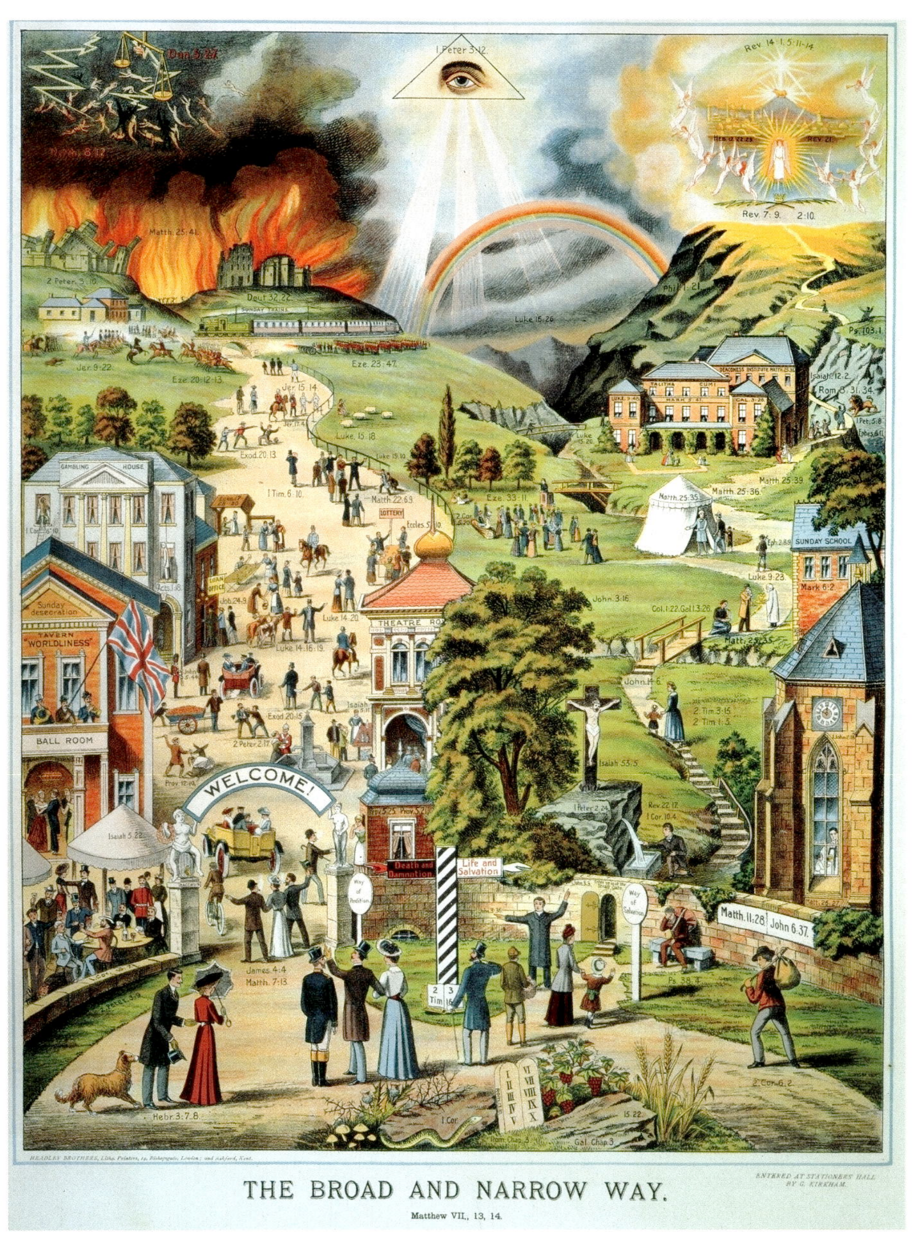

G.Kirkham (after Charlotte Reihlen), *The Broad and Narrow Way* (1883)

also conscious of working from a landscape tradition. The aesthetic of *Everglade* is deliberately painterly. The small figures moving through the scenes are like those added for colour in the background of 17th/18th century landscape painting, merely dots.

In 2002, I made a video piece called *No Evil Star* at the Hancock Museum in Newcastle. The Museum contains many of the stuffed birds that Bewick used as models for the series of woodcut bird illustrations, 'Bewick's Birds', that helped to make his name.

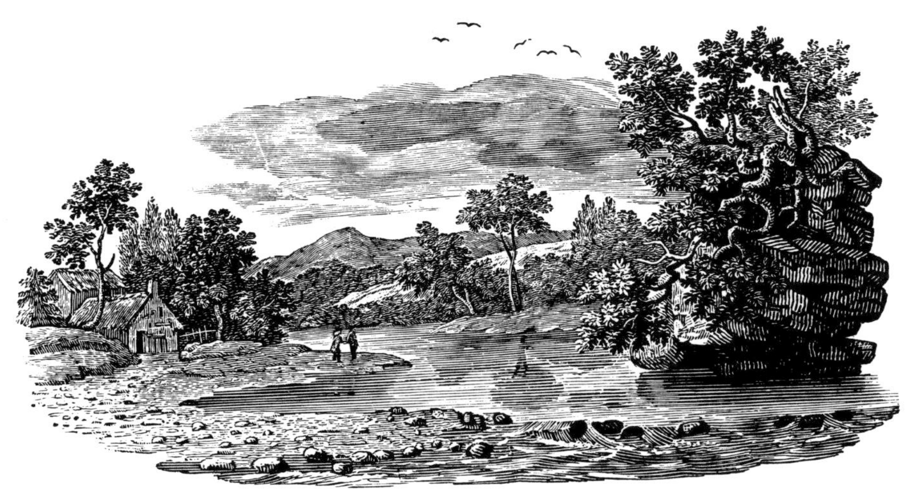

Much of Bewick's other work was landscapes and scenes of social life. Bewick didn't do otherworldly subjects, his imagery was everyday. But the vignette format is intrinsically visionary. It creates a deliberately fragmentary view, often minute in scale. It doesn't operate like the traditional window-on-the-world with clearly defined edges. Its edges are indeterminate, dependent on the features of the scene: the trees, the far hills, the useful clump of rock framing the view. With Bewick's landscapes there is no sense of continuation of the image, no sense that the frame is provisional. The landscape would

Woodcut by Thomas Bewick (*c.* 1800)

not continue to the right if you shifted slightly. I was drawn to the fact that the landscape was an object, like a blob, a pebble or a cloud. How it is shaped is defined by what is being depicted.

On a technical level I wasn't interested in making a film version of Bewick's images. The mark of a woodcut graphic and the pixellation of digital video are not comparable. But I wanted to make my filmed landscapes cohere and be believable as inhabited fictional spaces in the same way that Bewick's are.

Used in book illustration, the vignette lies in the middle of the page. The illumination within the image and the whiteness of the paper bleed into one another. In *Everglade*, the white light from the projector surrounding the image also forms the illumination within the scene. The screen operates like the single sheet of paper. You're conscious of the image as something made, something formed, being projected onto the screen.

Each filmed sequence becomes like a pictured or imaginary scene. In my images – unlike many of Bewick's – the sky is one of the main elements to go, and that has the biggest impact. There is no sky, all is land. What the sun does, we only see by reference to what happens on the ground. As the sun hides behind cloud, the scene plunges into darkness as if its power had been switched off. With the counterbalancing brightness of the whole sky gone, the projector does the work for the sun.

Isolated or framed as a vignette, the living world takes on the appearance of a model world, animated, making it seem sometimes entirely constructed. I like that ambiguity, and also the doubt as to whether the images are still or moving. In some scenes it can be hard to tell. So the provenance of the material is obscure. I think that's important.

The footage in *Everglade* is all filmed live. But drawing was one of the main elements in making the work — drawing over stills, editing through masking and then viewing footage through the mask. Masking is a device I've used elsewhere — *The Expressionists* being an obvious example and *Target Nebula* a more complex one.

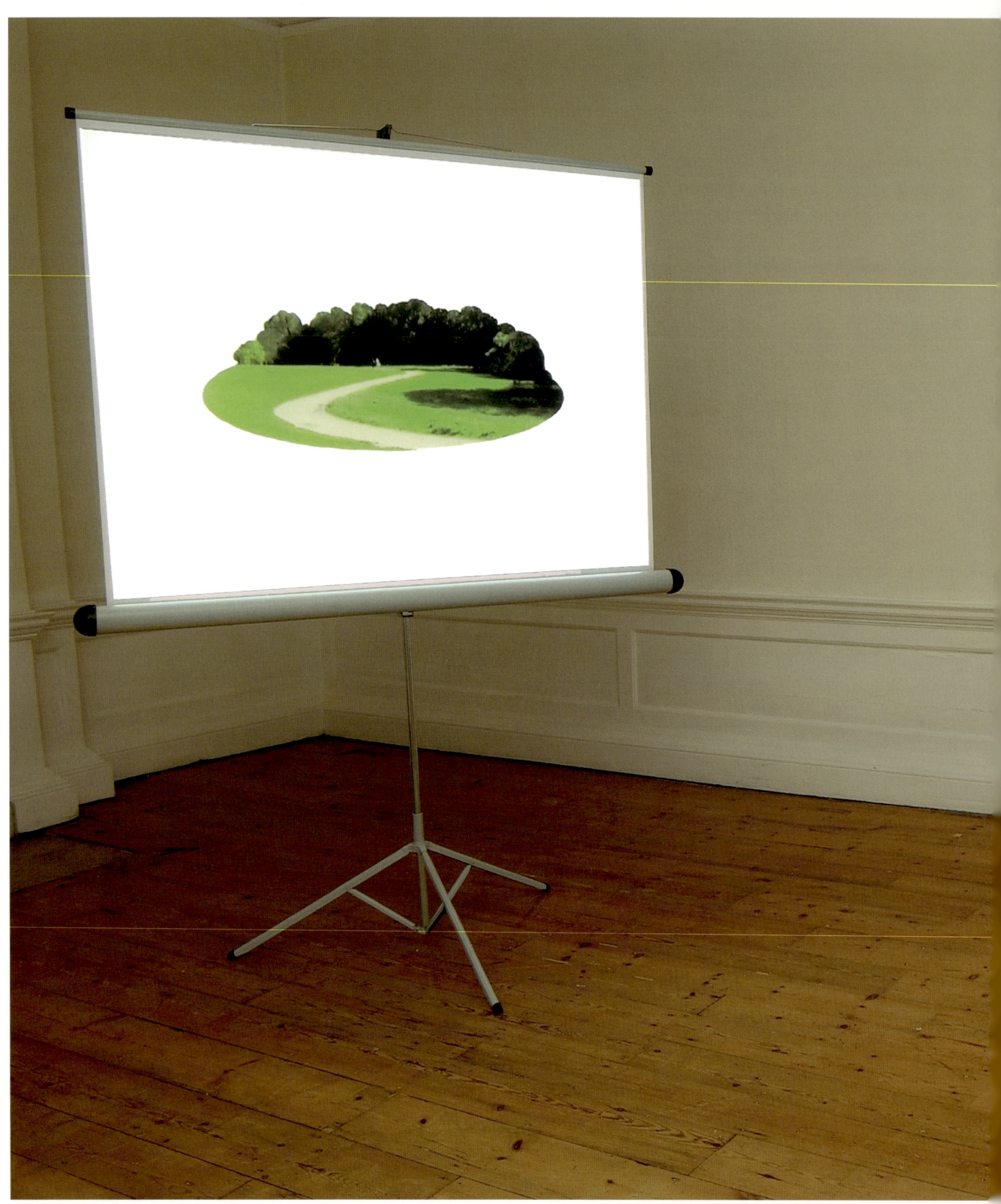

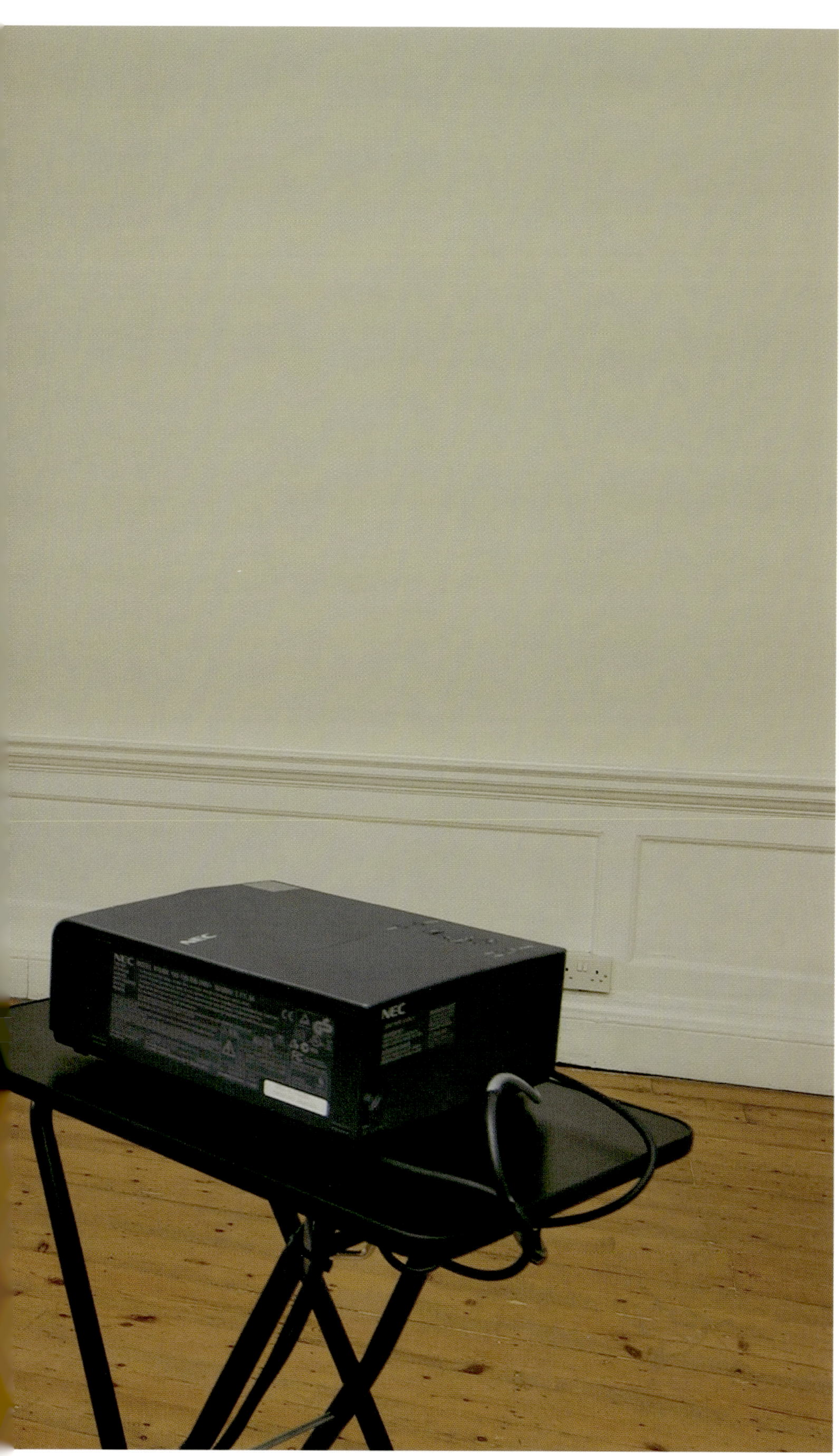

Everglade (2003)

In *Everglade* everything not wanted is masked out with white. The sky goes. The distant views go. Where-the-paths-go, goes. (The setting is a goal-less place, goals are for earth.) Likewise, within the action – which is very mundane, social activity, shot in parkland around London – the cyclists, kite-flyers, picnickers, baby-buggies, these all go. What I wanted to focus on was the paths themselves and the individuals using them. That kind of journeying, wandering at leisure, is directionless and self-contained. The figures travel through on their own or in pairs, two at the most can gather. All are representative, visible only at a distance, no one comes close enough for clarity.

The piece is designed to be seamless, suggesting that the activity is going on all the time. There are ten different scenes. The viewer can enter at any point. While working on it, the episodic aspect became more important within the structure — the rhythm of the suite of landscapes, the appearance of the figures, the duration of the white intervals between scenes. It all became more melancholic.

The intervals are long and are important for holding the pace. The fade to white is a filmic staple, often used to indicate cosmic or otherworldly experience, or a loss of consciousness. Fade to black is much more common. During these intervals the screen is pure white light, emphasising the work of the projector as a component in the piece, not just a part of the equipment. I wanted to link the projected light and the visionary nature of the image.

I like to expose the mechanics of the working of a piece, to make that part of the meaning — one reason why I don't automatically go for straight projections. *Assembly* projects a video image onto the top of a lectern, which puts the viewer in a one-to-one, reading relationship to the image, allowing an intimacy with something very grand in scale. *Everglade* was always intended as a sculptural piece. It is made up of a group of functional objects, a projector on a cross-legged stand, a projection screen on its tripod foot. Something about the provisionality of these structures made sense within the context of the piece. The relationship between this duo, screen and stand, was also important. The projector shoots at the screen, the screen bounces back the light. The visionary image is grounded in the prosaic, tethered to it like a balloon.

I'm always thinking about the different layers of experience, how the first encounter with the piece works, or how duration comes into it. With any gallery projection there's always the question, how long do you stay and watch, when do you decide to leave? That uncertainty is part of the experience.

Both *epic* and *No Evil Star* have definite beginnings and ends. In a way those pieces each contain a process – in *epic* it's an onward journey, in *No Evil Star*, a fading of light – that is heading towards an end. Watching the projection is an act of waiting. In *Cult* you entered into a relationship with a group of faces on a number of screens which could never be taken in whole; you stood amongst them, but at some point you had to leave the group, breaking this relationship. With *Everglade* it's different again, you're standing amongst the apparatus. There isn't a correct viewing position for the viewer. There is almost a private relationship between the projector and the image, with the viewer as onlooker. You have a perspective on it but you can't really lose yourself in it. Yet the piece has its own absorbing rhythm, it goes on, people pass through, the images fade, the sequences repeat, it could go on forever.

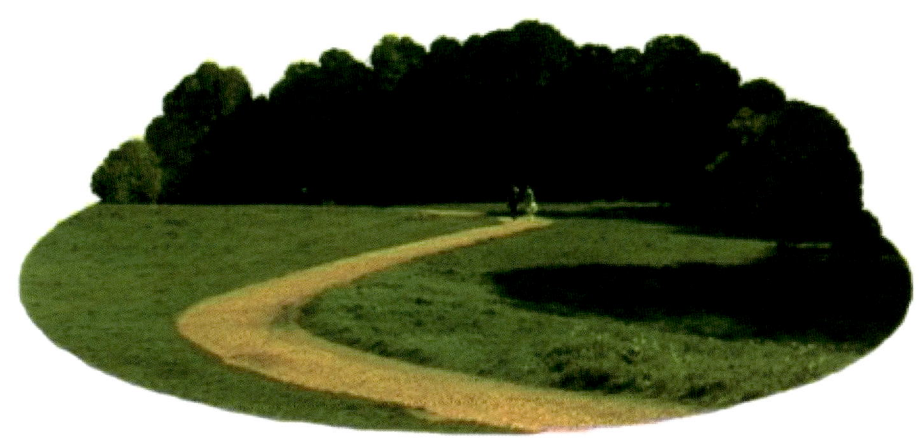

Prophet (2003)

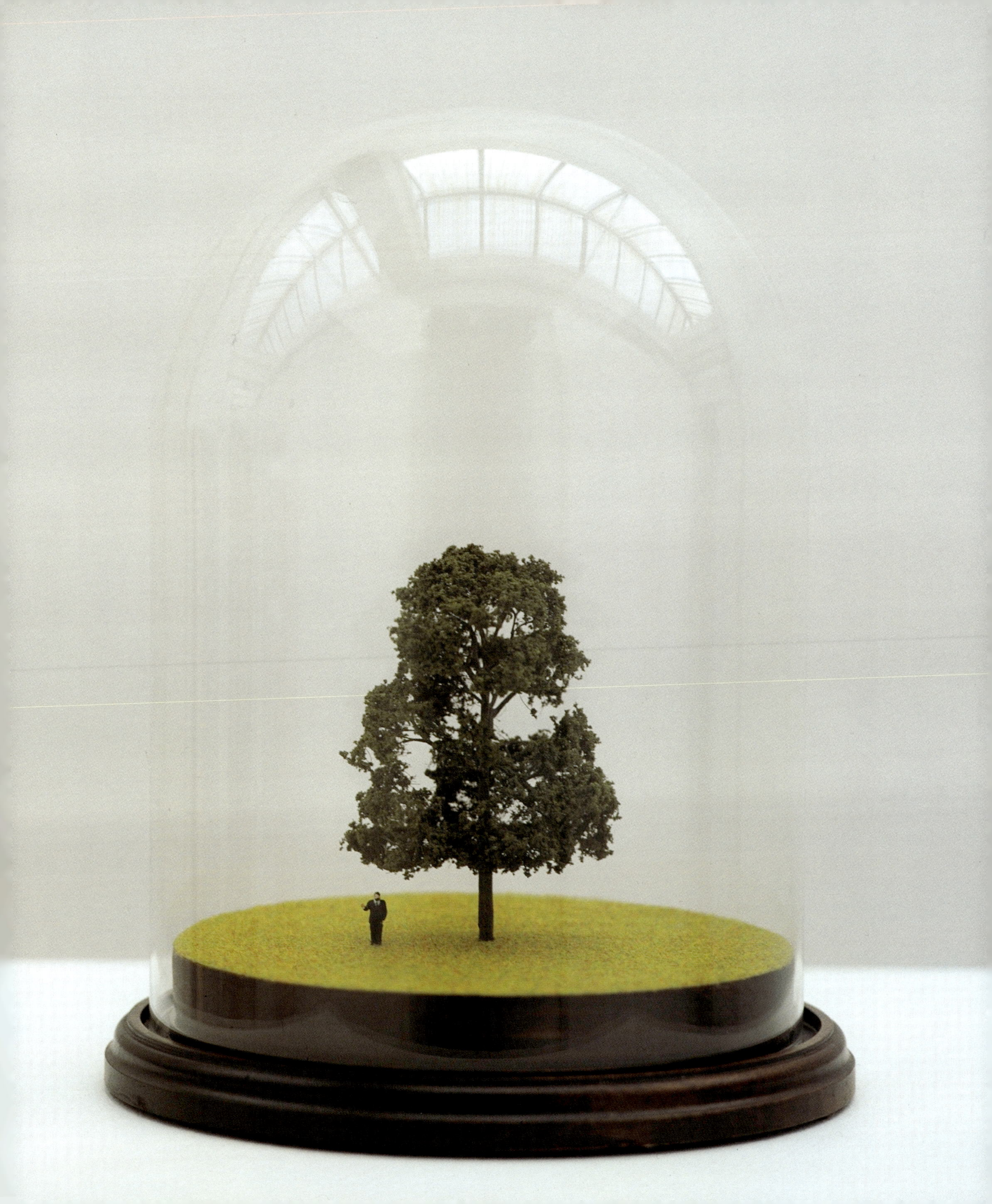

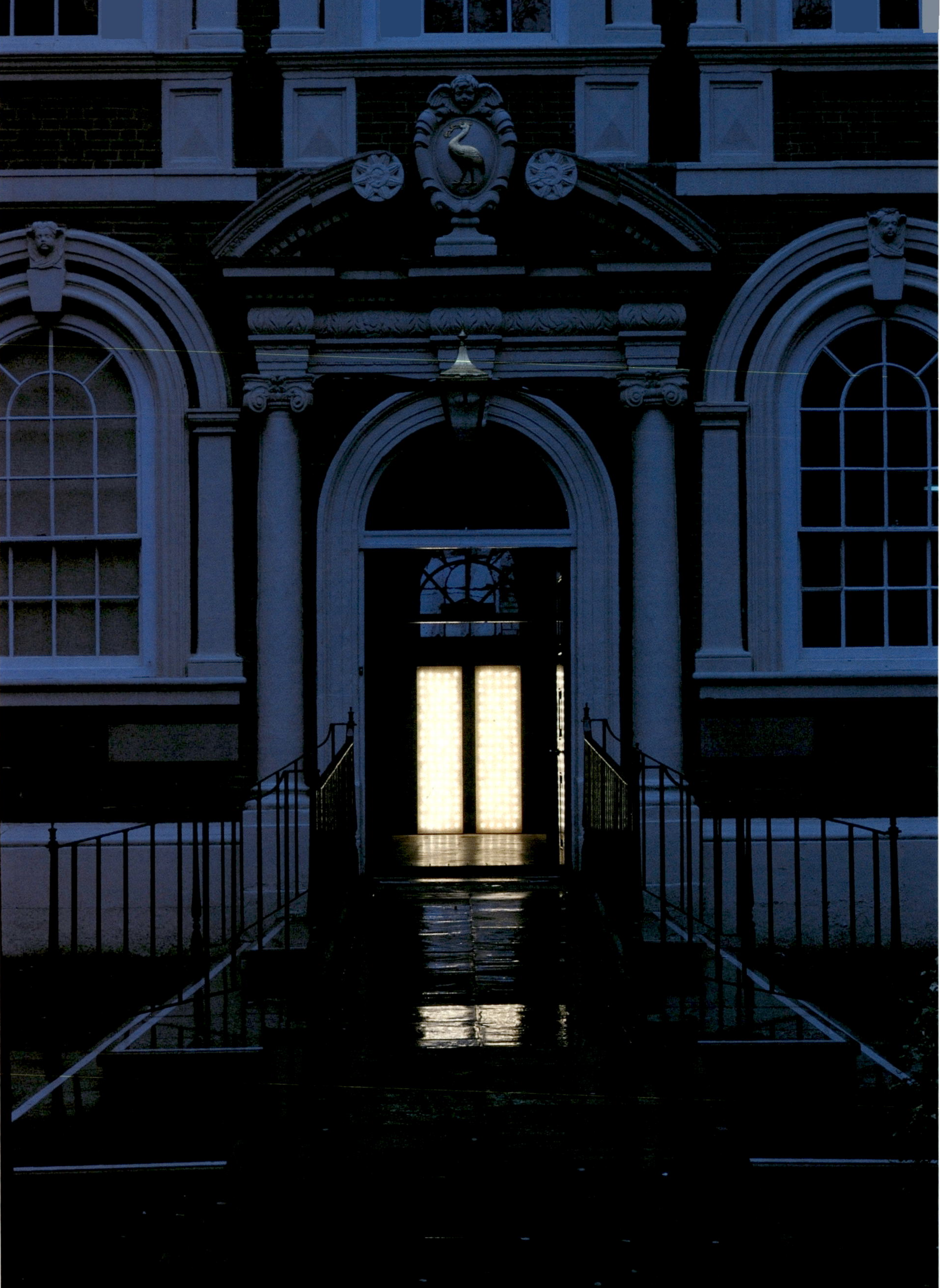

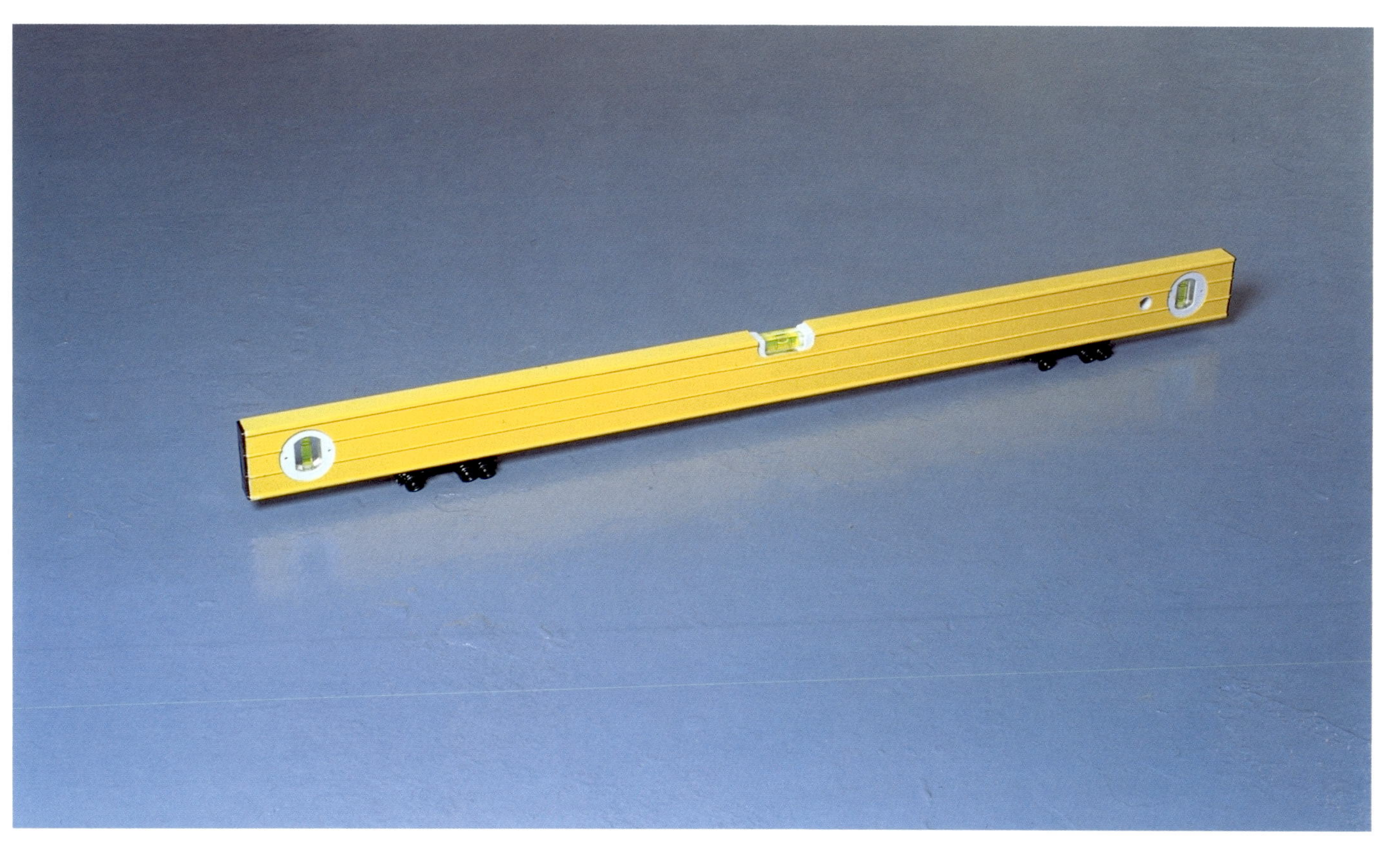

Palace (2001), installation Bluecoat Gallery, Liverpool

Untilted (2003)

Decalogue (2001)

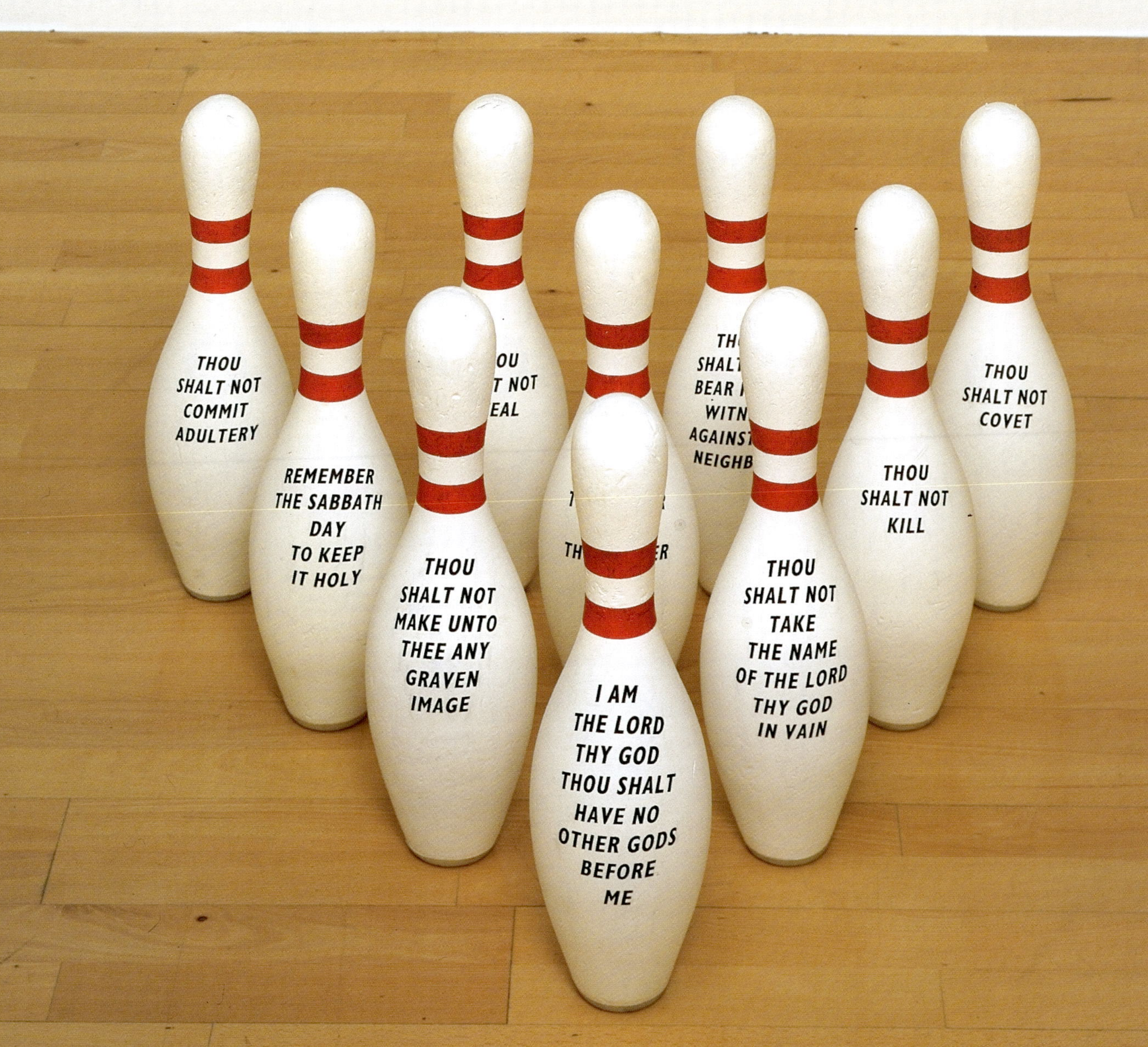
THOU SHALT NOT COMMIT ADULTERY
REMEMBER THE SABBATH DAY TO KEEP IT HOLY
THOU SHALT NOT MAKE UNTO THEE ANY GRAVEN IMAGE
THOU SHALT NOT STEAL
I AM THE LORD THY GOD THOU SHALT HAVE NO OTHER GODS BEFORE ME
THOU SHALT NOT BEAR FALSE WITNESS AGAINST THY NEIGHBOUR
THOU SHALT NOT TAKE THE NAME OF THE LORD THY GOD IN VAIN
THOU SHALT NOT KILL
THOU SHALT NOT COVET

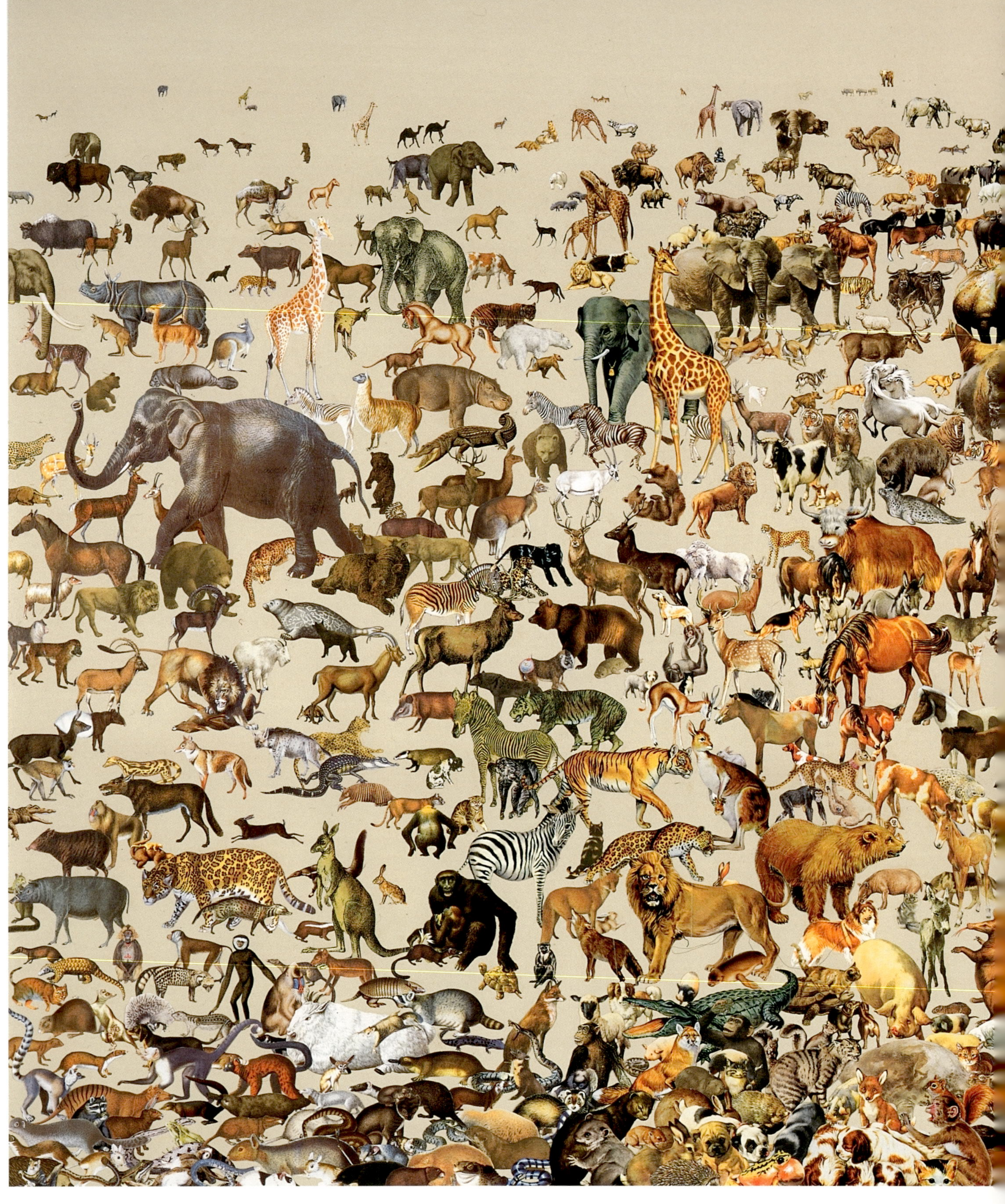

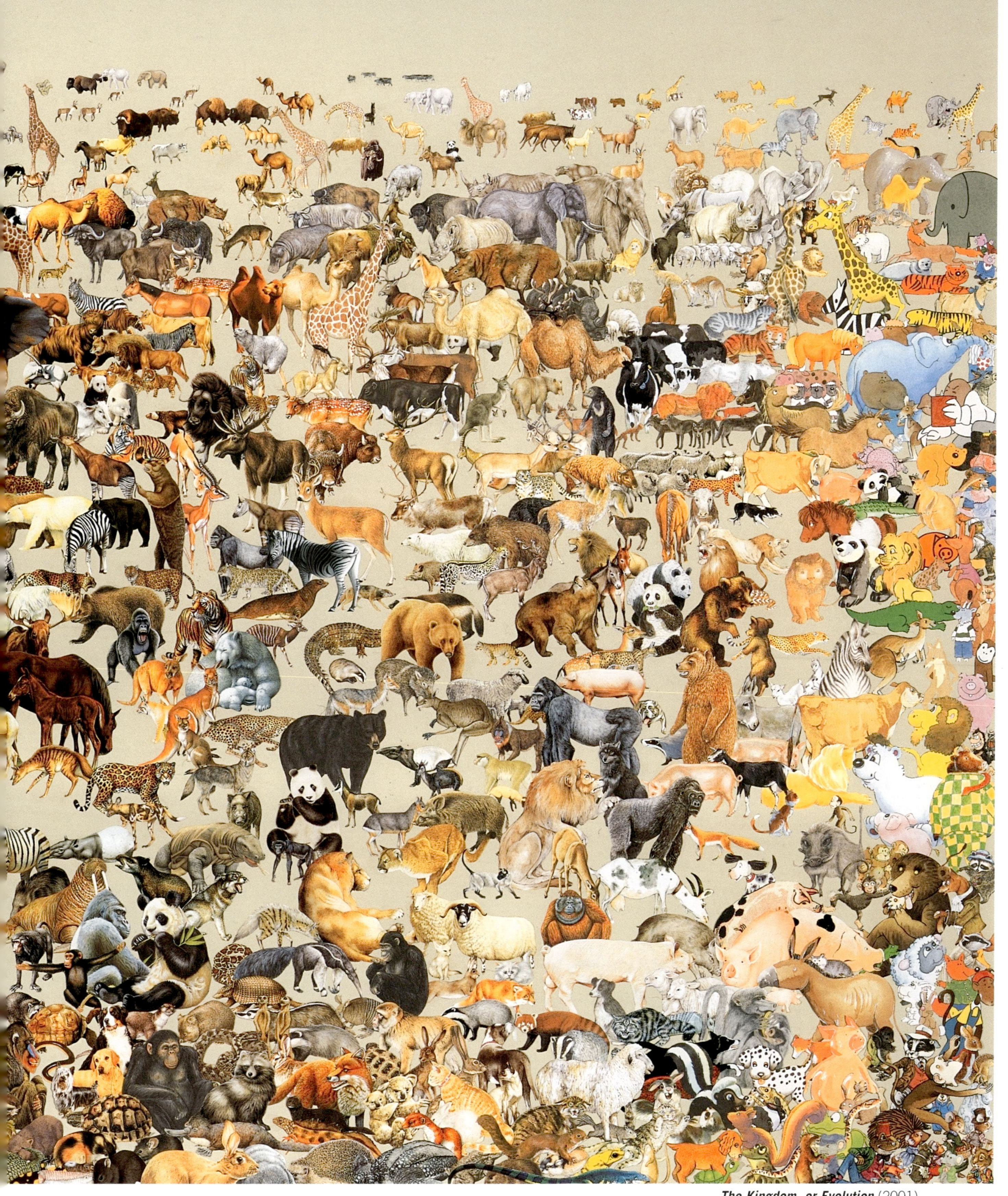

The Kingdom, or Evolution (2001)

Key (to The Kingdom, or Evolution) (2001)

Where we live

Vincent Deary

Urban planners and landscape architects describe a phenomenon they call 'natural desire lines' or simply 'desire lines'. Our local park has one, a foot-worn rut connecting both ends of the scenic curve of the official path like the string of an archery bow. The public have voted with their feet, chosen expediency over prescribed detour and stamped their intention onto the landscape. There is even a desire line urban myth, a fable of peak planning practice. An American college campus is sown with lawns and left unpaved for a year — only then are the natural routes that people make through it given the official endorsement of paving. What is intriguing about this process is that it manifests the spontaneous, unplanned desire of a collective over time. One can imagine how, given a slight alteration in the initial conditions, the path might have been different, but once the first suggestion is adopted it becomes a matter of public record, gets used again and again, until it becomes the quasi-official established route. The path that we give rise to in turn directs our movement, becomes our collective memory.

This joint establishment and performance of social routines is a recurring theme in Marion Coutts' work. Lazily, we tend to think of customs, rituals and communal habits as residing in some abstract collective unconscious. What Coutts draws our attention to is the fact that these routines are embodied, that our social memory is recorded in the shapes our communal activity has inscribed on the landscape. Take *Fresh Air*, in which the distinctive outlines of three of London's parks define the shapes and markings of three asymmetrical (but playable) table-tennis tables. *Fresh Air* evokes the idea of the public space, the leisure park, as a circumscribed game, a place with its own set of rules, its own routines and rituals. "Different parks offer different games," reads one of Coutts' notes to the work. The park is at the same time both the map and the

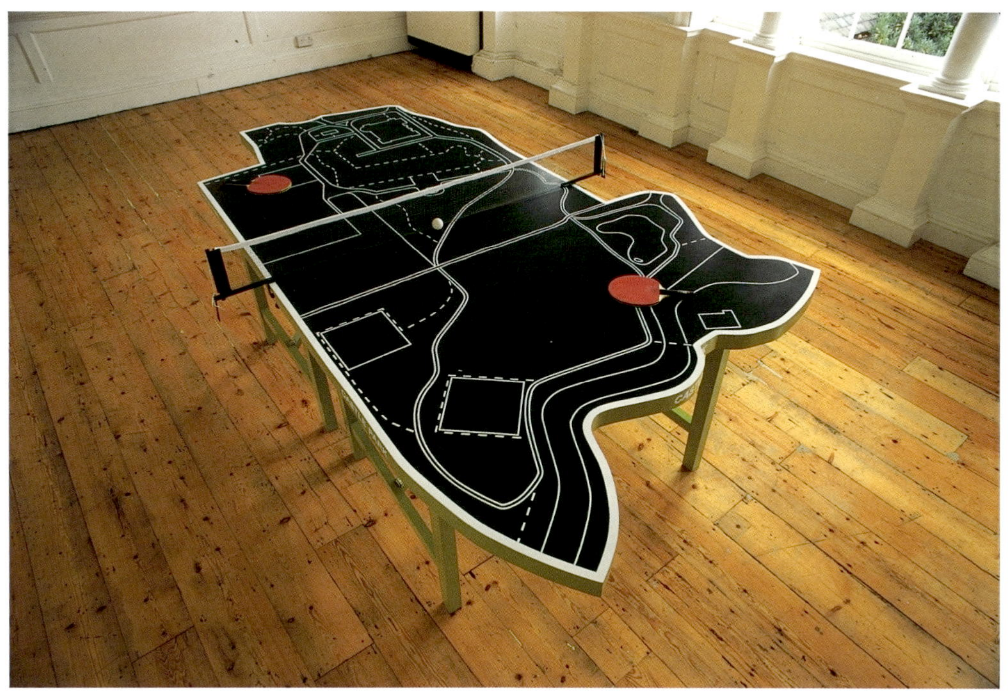

Castle Park (2000)

territory of enjoyment; this public space is our shared memory of the solved problems
of leisure. A similar idea informs *Everglade* in which Coutts, using the filmic equivalent
of the pictorial vignette, isolates the subroutines of park life. The individuals within
them are anonymous units, following the guidelines of recreation. It is almost as if the
park is taking them for a walk.

And this is what we want routines to do. No coincidence that 'a walk in the park' is
a synonym for ease. We don't read the choreography of the path, we don't practice
the action of the fruit machine, we do them. A path leads us and we follow, we place
ourselves on the ride and it runs. Similarly, many other sets of circumstance – the
wedding, the fairground, the gym, the penny arcade, the cinema, the club – are social
objects, strange attractors we are drawn to, commune in and through. Like actors
replacing a character in a twenty-year West End run, we enter the mousetraps of public
routine. There is little to think about. Leisure is precisely this: the switching off of decision,
of choice and doubt. We place ourselves in environments where routine runs us.

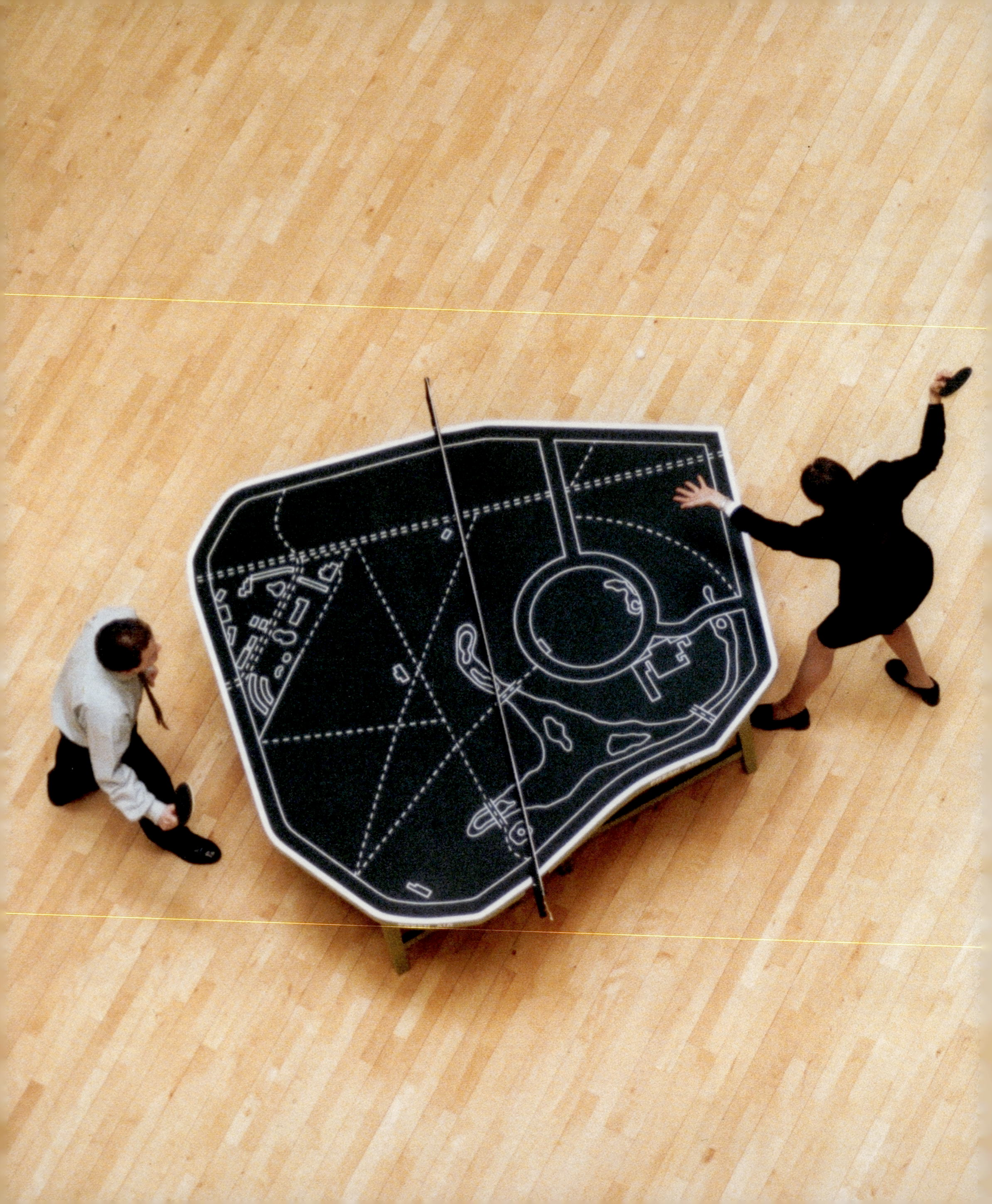

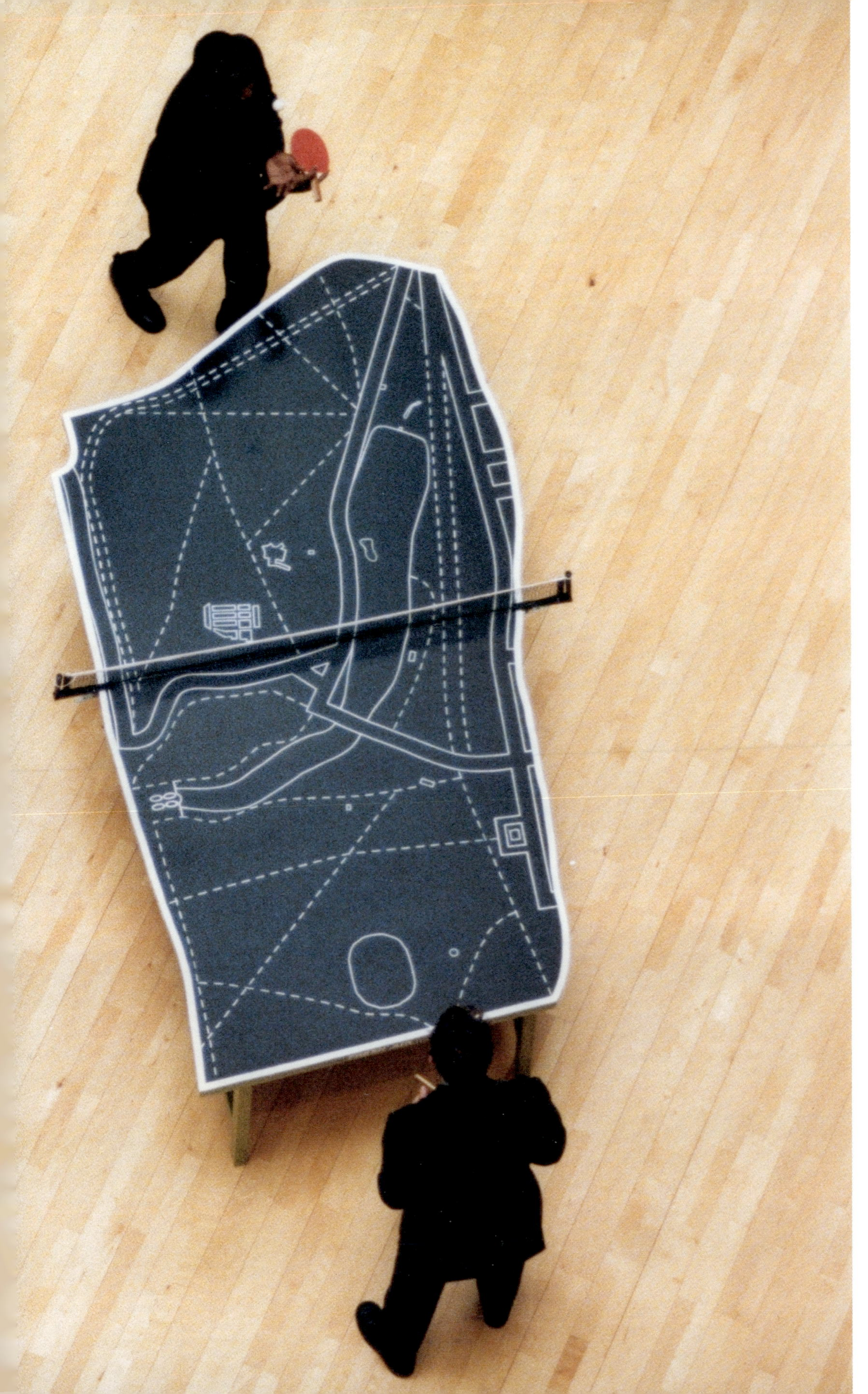

Fresh Air (1998–2000)

But there is also something creepy here. Benign or not, there is a kind of possession at work, an abdication of will to a larger agency. The individual, like the starling in the flock, is a unit of an impersonal process. FOR THE FALLEN, the inscription carved on the gym horse totem of institutional P.E., reminds of us the backs that are broken on the rack of routine. And then there is *Break*, the most unsettling of Coutts' works, in which three hamsters are set free from their cages into 'playballs', completely enclosed transparent spheres. Regardless of where they want to go, they go, but the spheres that contain them move with them. The spheres, the billiard-ball geometry of the process, have a momentum of their own. Bumbling relentlessly into the borders of their world, into each other, the circumscribed freedom of each sphere is itself circumscribed by the physics of the situation and the movement of the others. Like an animal Beckett play, *Break* offers the most condensed, most exquisitely ambiguous metaphor for living. Watching it, we can decide that this is cruel, or that their semi-willed hurtling is exhilarating, their theme park joy-ride. We can choose to see them happy or sad, caged or free.

In the same way, our living occurs within an established and overarching order, and our relationship to our place(s) within that order is profoundly ambivalent. There is an old story we continually re-tell, where the socio-symbolic matrix, the 'system' in which we are immersed, is the source of oppression and the hero's defining characteristics are rebellion and subversion. Usually in this story, the system is overthrown, transformed or escaped; occasionally, Big Brother like, it wins. In this light, we might celebrate the spirit of revolution as a refusal to walk the desire lines of posterity, as an attempt to forge and walk new ones. The rebellious spirit is pioneering, groundbreaking, romantic. Put this way, who wants to be a cog? But Coutts complicates this. We are as complicit as we are coerced. Our self-reflexivity, our motivational complexity, assures that apart from the most basic mass behaviour, the co-ordination of human being requires a set of prescribed routines, moves and roles, props and scripts. Oppression may be there, but so are the possibilities of liberation and leisure and the machinery for communication. Could we live without them?

Coutts' installation *Assembly* presents an example of a living unmediated by ideology. Or seems to. Projected onto a lectern, like a sacred text, a video image of a flight of starlings moves back and forth, a spookily coherent massing (the collective nouns for which include both a 'concentration' and a 'constellation'). There is a unity of purpose

Break (2000)

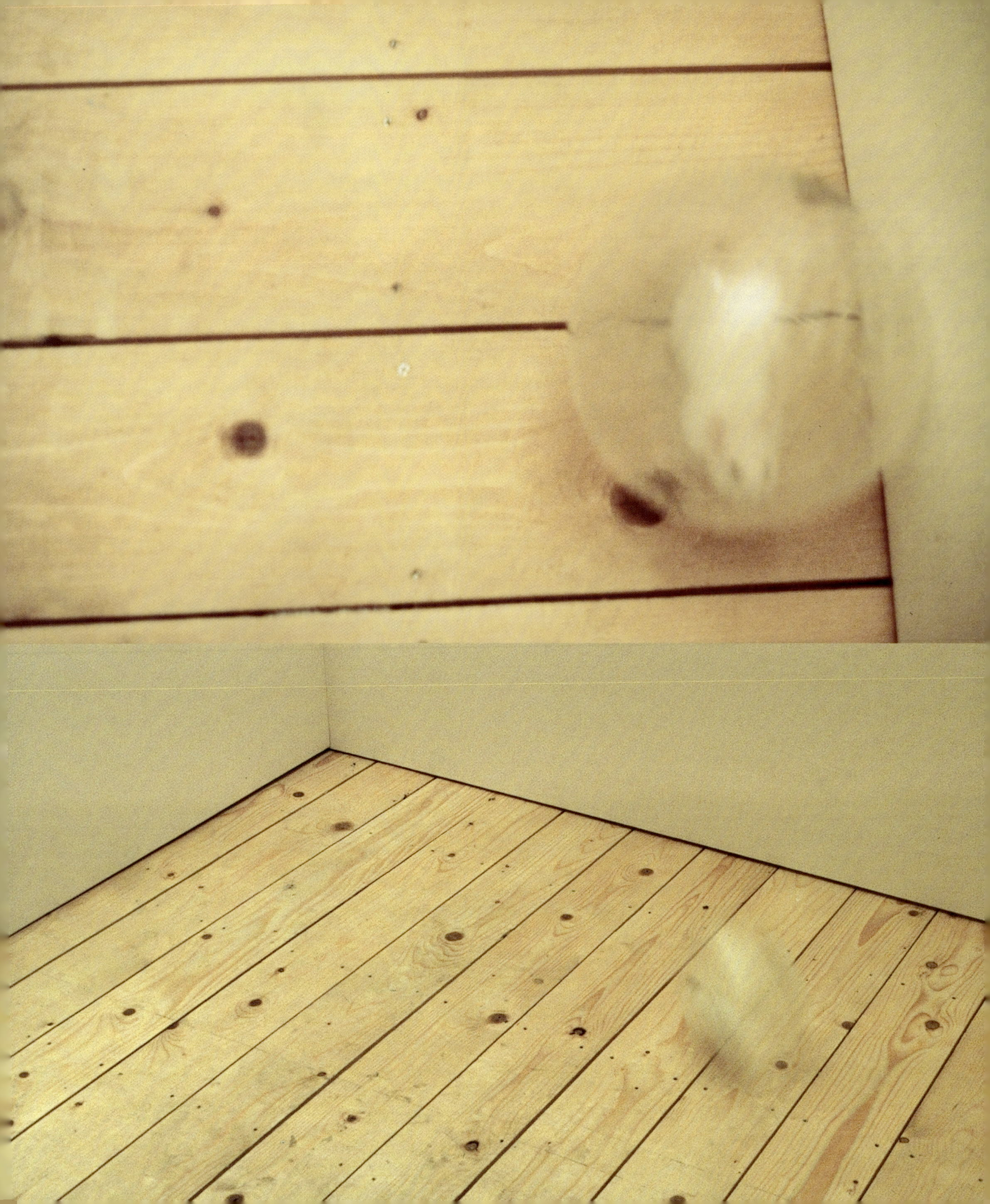

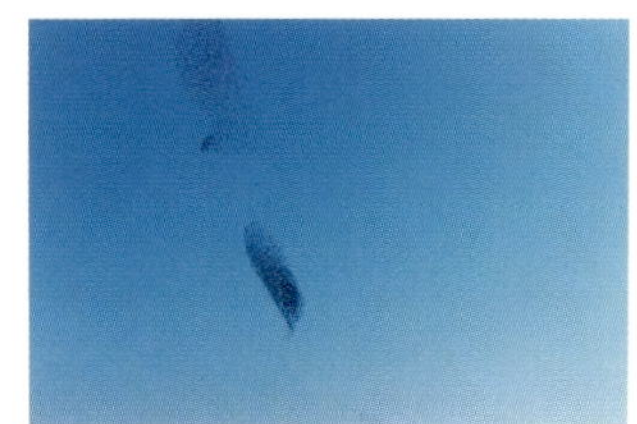

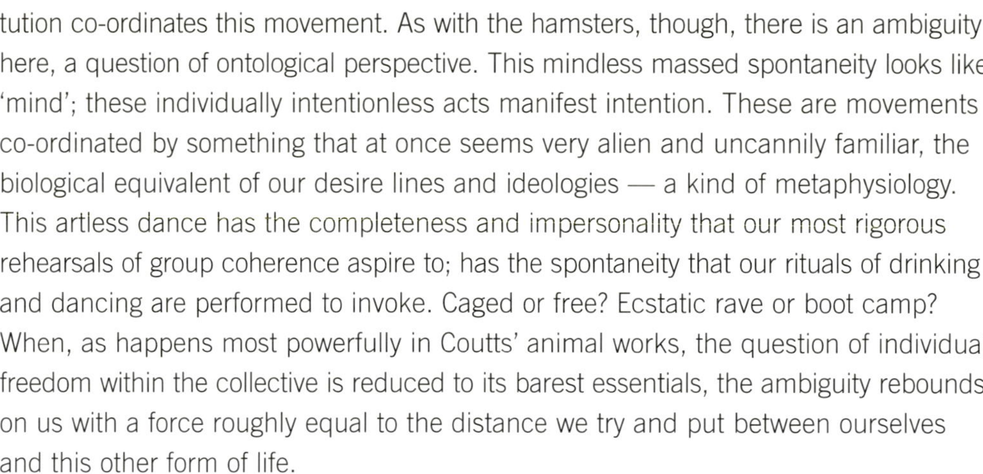

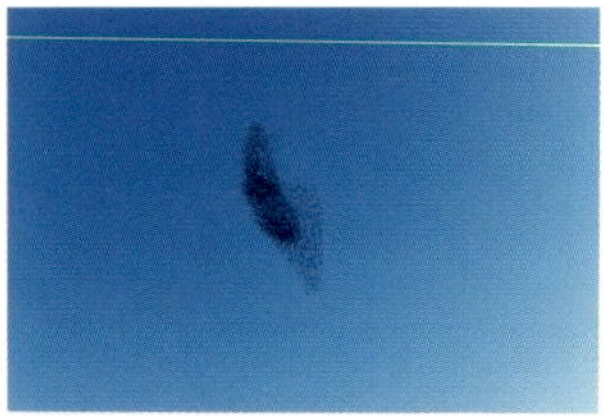

of such immediacy that the process seems truly miraculous. No consultation, no institution co-ordinates this movement. As with the hamsters, though, there is an ambiguity here, a question of ontological perspective. This mindless massed spontaneity looks like 'mind'; these individually intentionless acts manifest intention. These are movements co-ordinated by something that at once seems very alien and uncannily familiar, the biological equivalent of our desire lines and ideologies — a kind of metaphysiology. This artless dance has the completeness and impersonality that our most rigorous rehearsals of group coherence aspire to; has the spontaneity that our rituals of drinking and dancing are performed to invoke. Caged or free? Ecstatic rave or boot camp? When, as happens most powerfully in Coutts' animal works, the question of individual freedom within the collective is reduced to its barest essentials, the ambiguity rebounds on us with a force roughly equal to the distance we try and put between ourselves and this other form of life.

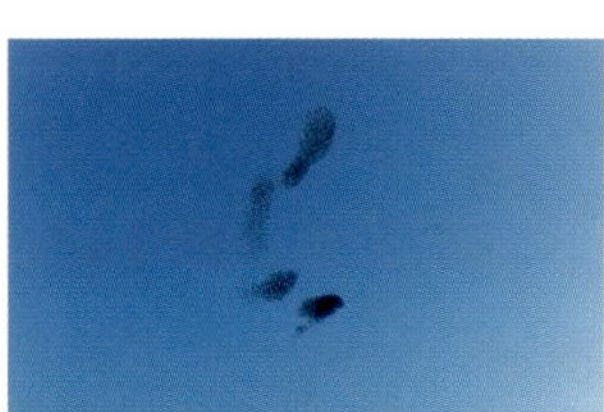

No greater distance surely than from the life of the worm. Coutts' *No Evil Star* is a short and epic wide-screen film with a cast of thousands of mealworms. Commonly used as anglers' bait and bought by the bucketload, they are at the opposite end of the food chain. But in this film they rule the earth. Set on a miniature mountainous diorama that makes them look gigantic, they thrive and writhe under the alien sun, worm-gods in Olympian orgy. Mealworms are photokinetic, so as the light begins to die their striving slowly ceases. As twilight cedes to darkness, all movement stops and the worms glimmer coldly like a field of the fallen. From hamsters to starlings to worms, there is a declension of complexity of behaviour and a concomitant increase in the universality of its form — like life being seen from a greater, then a greater distance, until eventually its essential shape becomes apparent. And that shape is the Day.

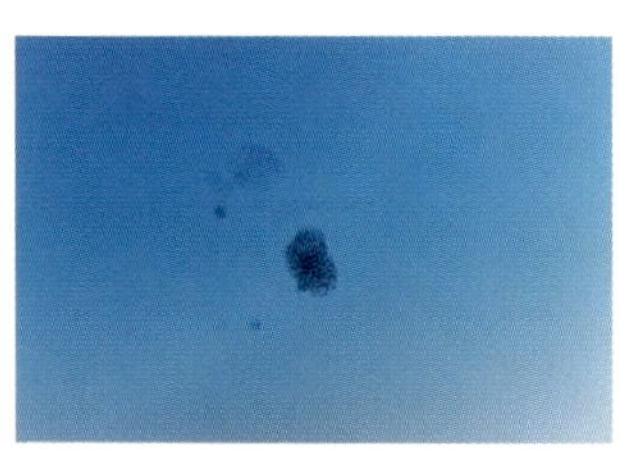

Our living, all sub-solar life, takes place within the universal proscenium arch of the Day. Days are inescapable, we rue and treasure them, live and die in them. Seen from a great enough distance our living does not look so different from the worms: stirring and striving with the light, then succumbing to the universal truce of sleep at night. No matter their content, Days set a universal rhythm to which we all move. As our most fundamental rhythm, our ur-cycle, it is also the most resonant. Many of our myths and numinous symbols trace the arc of the birth, death and rebirth of the light. We talk about the dawn of civilisations, the twilight years of individual lifetimes. The Day is our universal unit of measurement, and also of meaning. Not only days, but all narratives

Augury (2000)

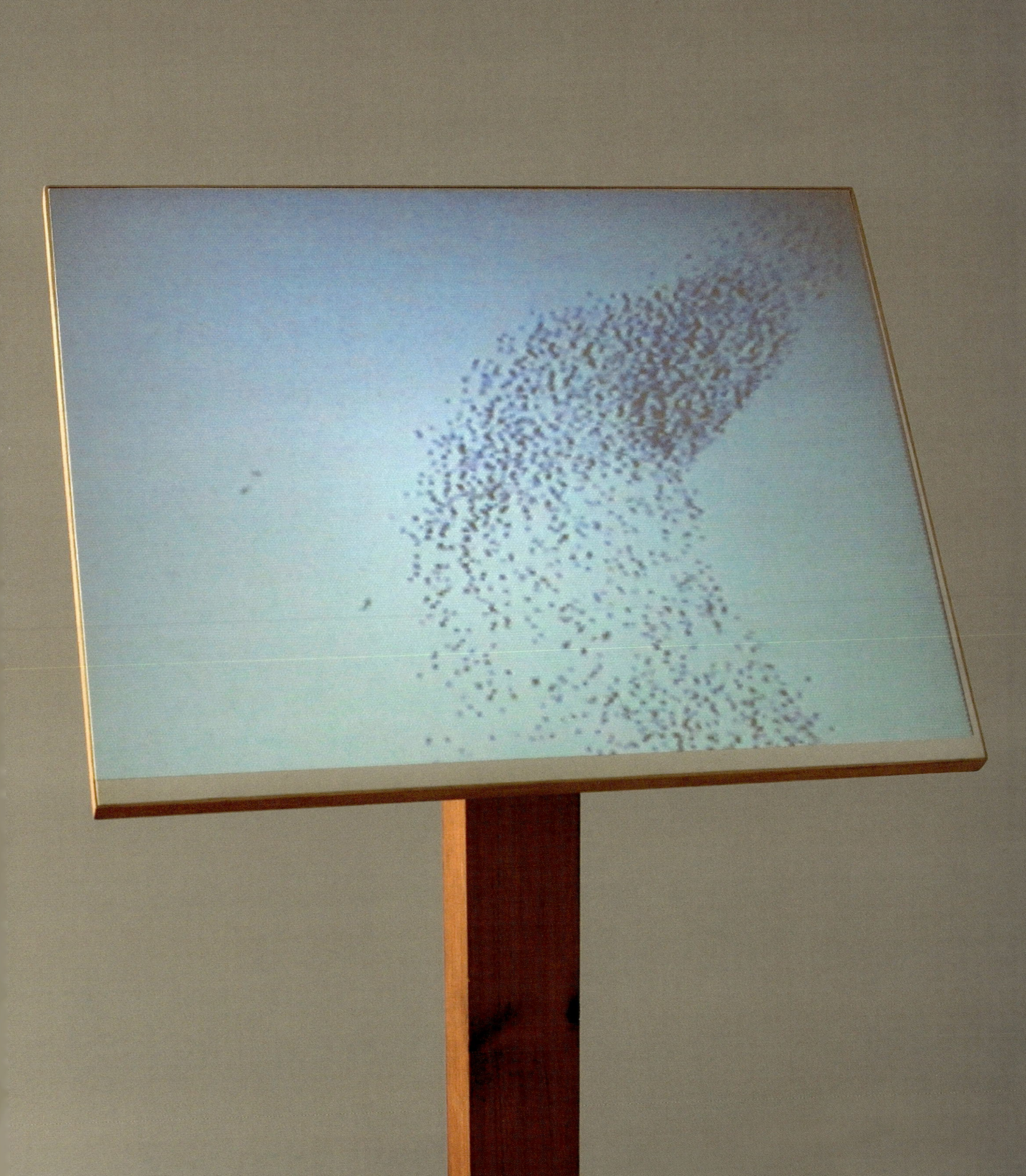

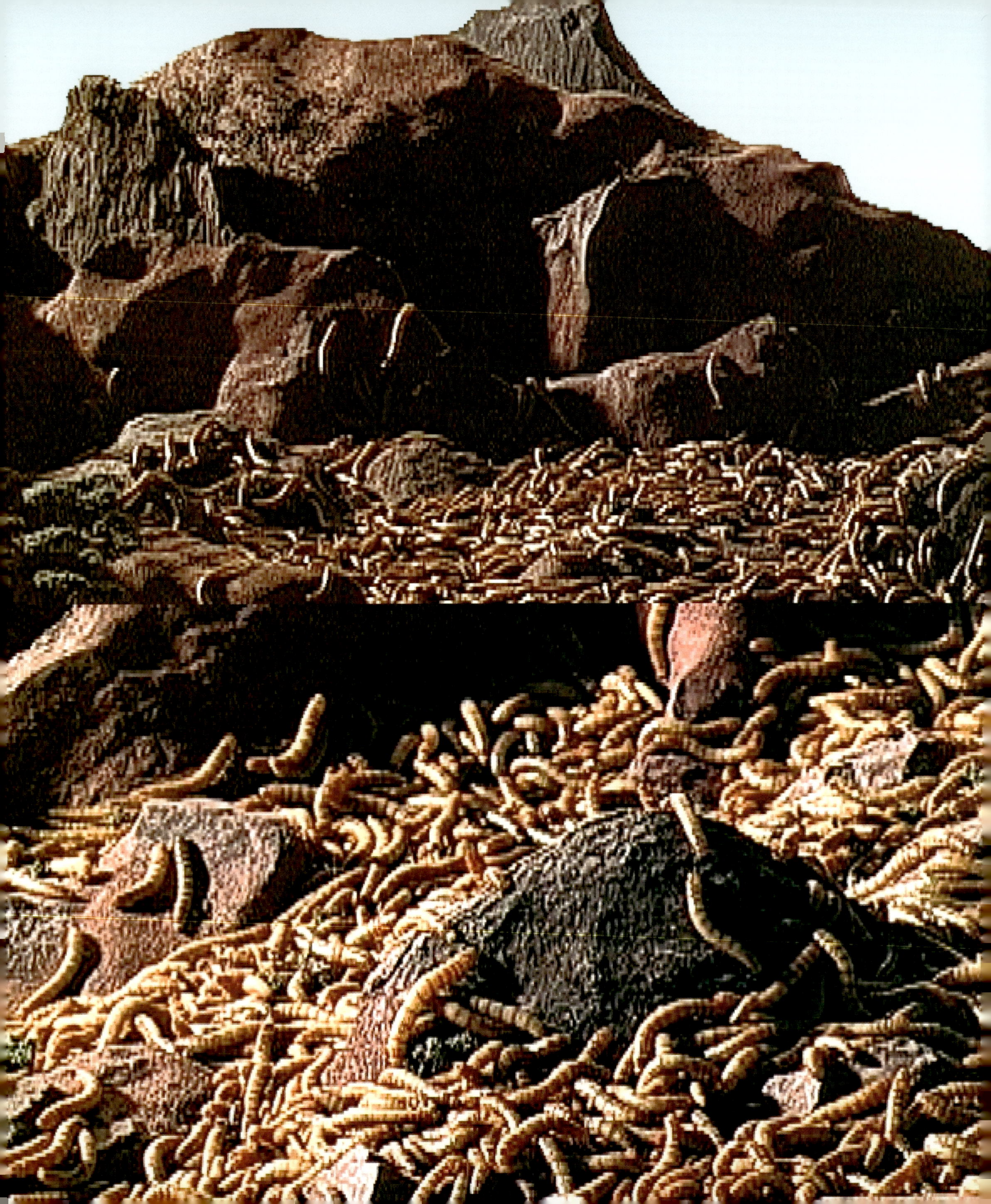

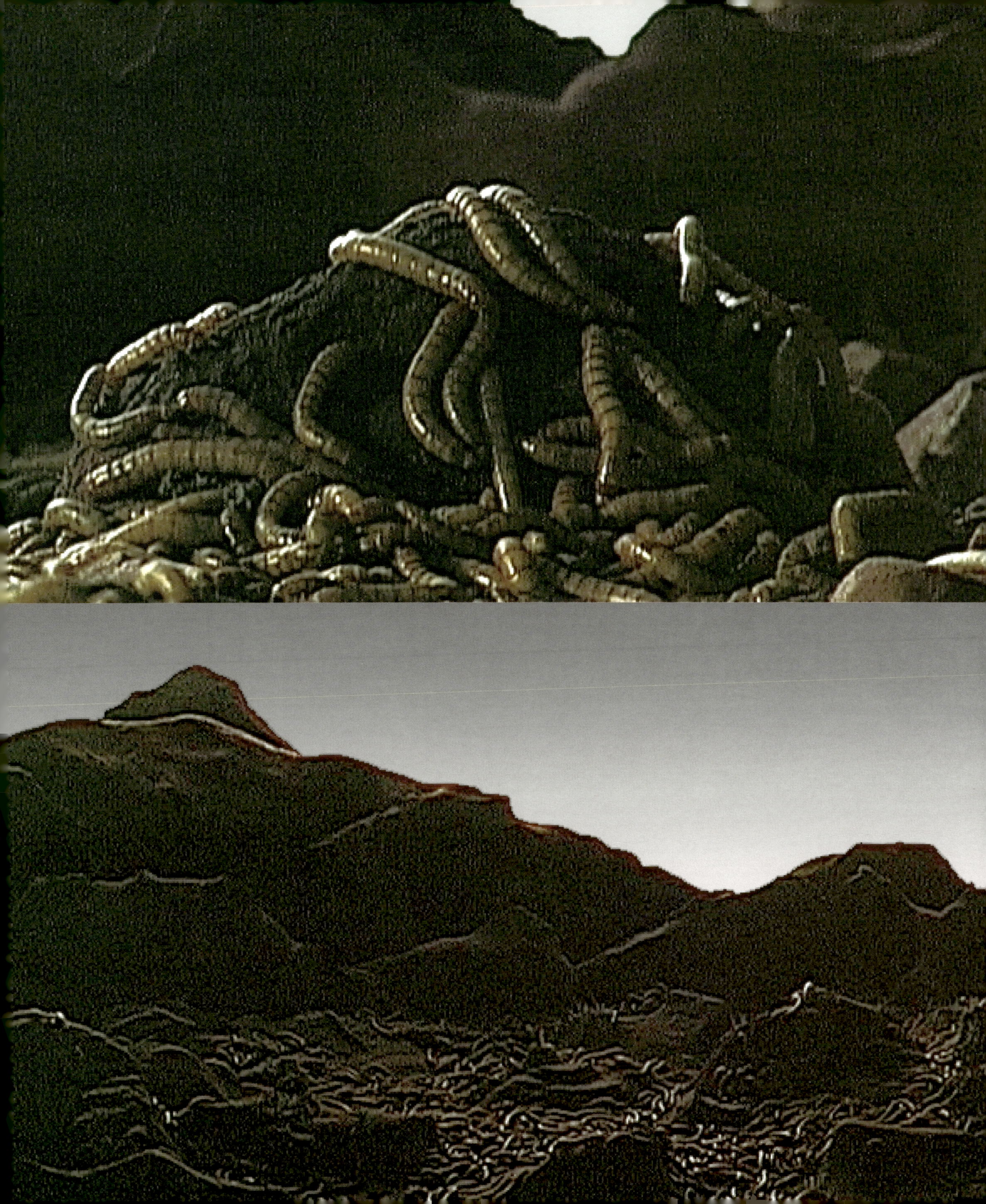

(be they of lives or epochs), make sense once they have ended, once we can trace the path of their rise and fall, once we can see their final shape. These worms could be enacting the end of a civilisation or just another day. The shape would be the same.

We seem to have come a long way from our walk in the park. There is no easy synthesis of the points covered, for that is not what Coutts' work is about. Rather, step by step and piece by piece, Coutts maps some of the places where we live, highlights some of the rules of our different games. You could order these rules in a hierarchy of givenness, from the environmental to the biological through to the social and contractual, to the more or less personal and consensual, to those we do for fun. She touches on each. And there is something implicit — there are always other games and places, but there is never an end of them. The notion of an elsewhere, an outside, a place without place — we glimpse it in *Everglade*. The isolated film-vignettes of park life are projected onto a pristine white projection screen, its luminous blankness lights and delineates, frames and grounds the scene. Our living takes place within that frame. As the film moves on, we return to the same places in the park. Different figures and weather move across them, but, stark against the nothingness that surrounds them, their shape acquires a kind of memorial constancy, a sculptural solidity. The strange reciprocity between our world and us has carved these shapes. The light changes, and slowly, from the left, a new character walks into the scene, another little drama is enacted.

previous page: **No Evil Star** (2002)

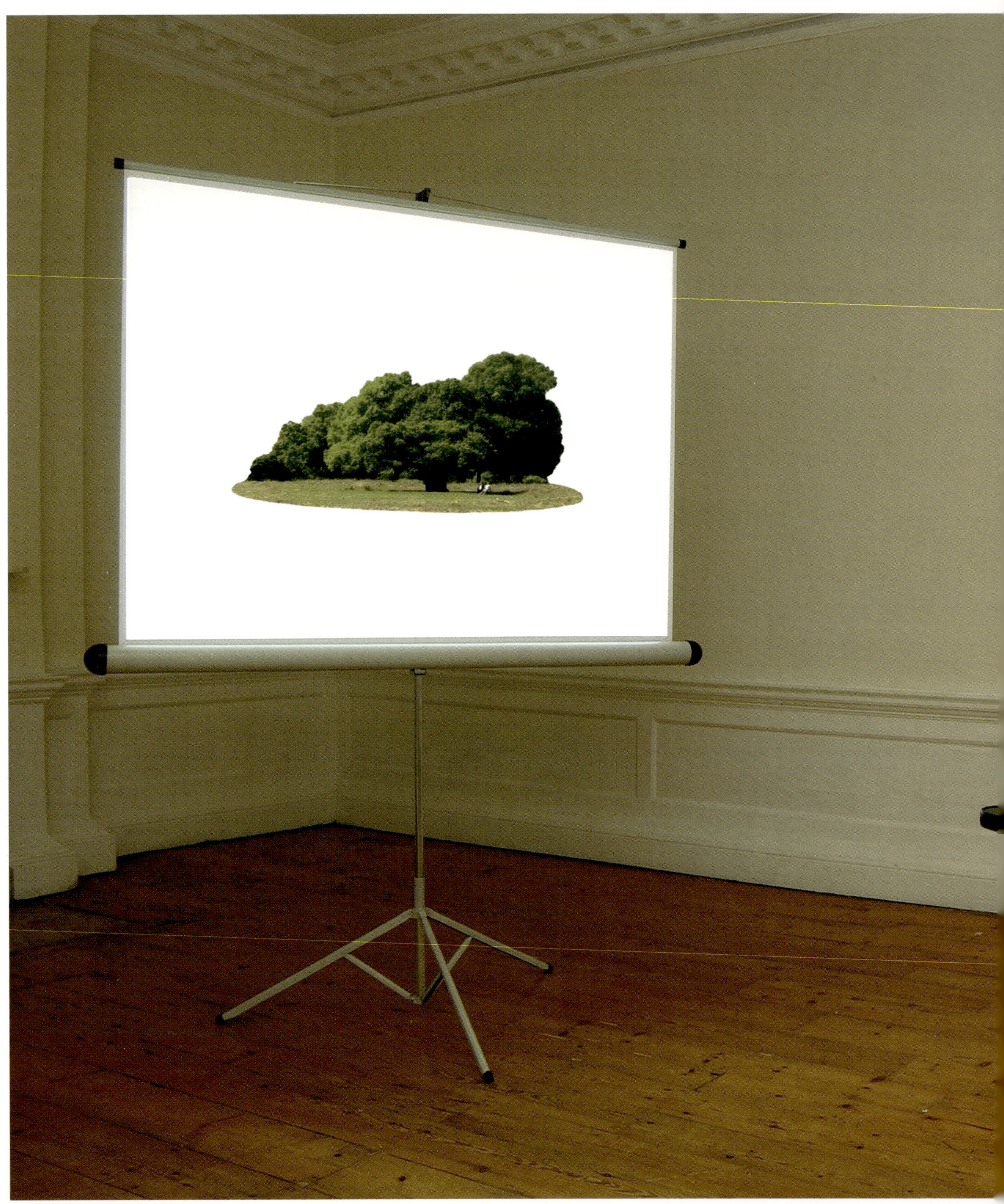

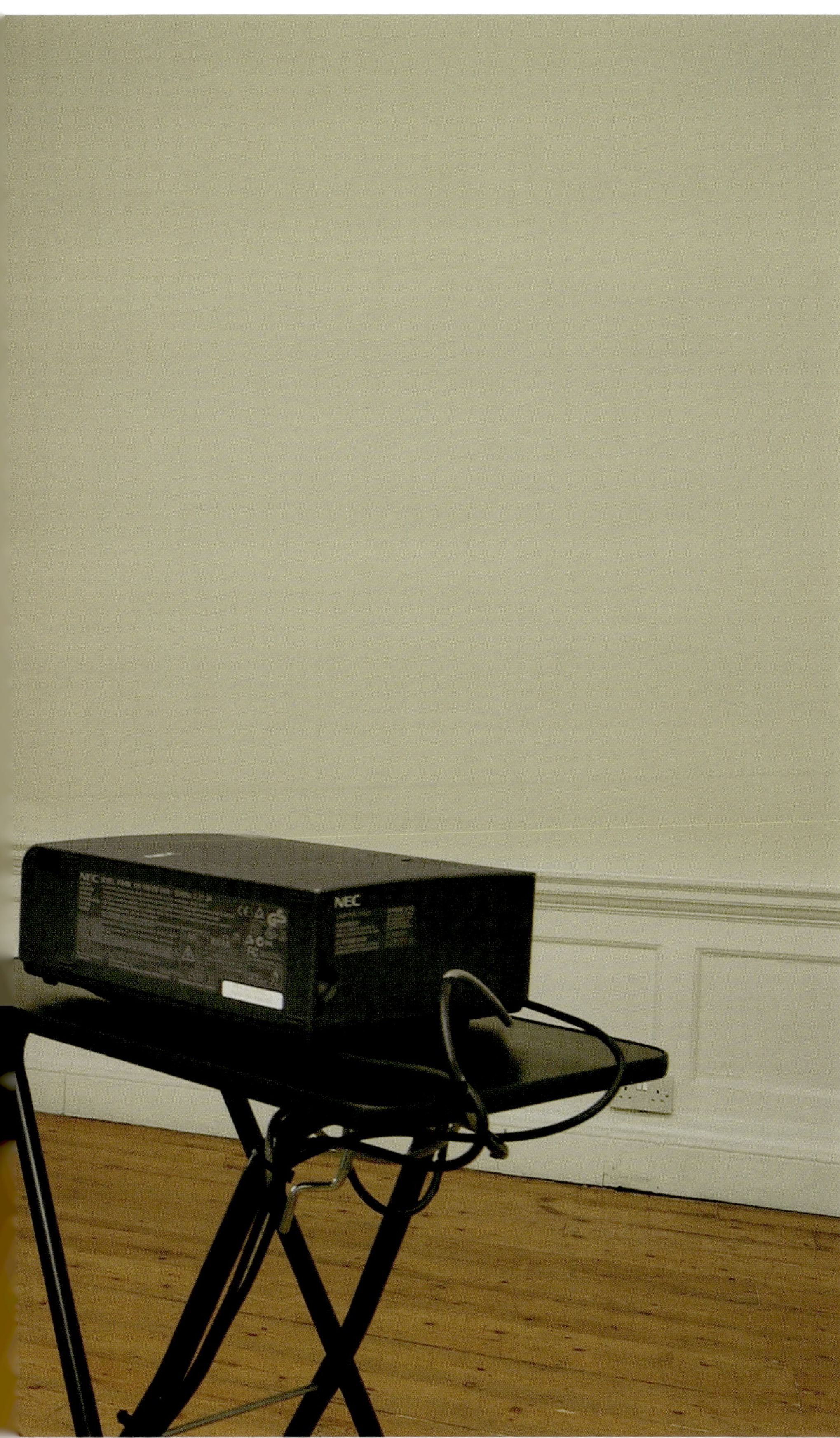

Everglade (2003)

List of works

Everglade (2003)
Installation: digital video on DVD,
projector, screen, stand
duration 10 mins on continuous loop
Screen size 116 x 152 cm
pp 6–7, 32–33, 58–59

Target Nebula (2003)
Ink, archery target
125 x 125 cm
p 8 and cover

Some Enchanted Evening (2001)
Jeweller's ring-liners, wood, wedding rings
122 x 250 cm
pp 11, 12–13

Sibyl (2001)
Satellite dish, stand, veil
230 cm high
p 14

The Expressionists (2001)
Televisions, paint, plinths
34.2 x 33.4 x 33 cm, 35.5 x 35.5 x 33 cm,
plinths 100 cm high
pp 16, 17

Cult (2002)
Installation at Chisenhale Gallery:
nine 9" monitors, plinths, podium,
DVDs on continuous loop
Dimensions variable
pp 18, 19

For the Fallen (2001)
Wood, suede, padding
110 x 125 x 120 cm
p 21

Money (2003)
1p coins, plaster, modelling wax
Dimensions variable
pp 23, 25

epic (2000)
Super 8 on DVD
duration 12 mins
soundtrack by Andy Moor and
Anna McMichael
pp 26, 27

Prophet (2003)
Bell jar, wood, model tree and grass, figure
32 cm high, 25.5 cm diameter
p 37

Palace (2001)
Lightbulbs, wood, sockets, paint
Dimensions variable
boxes 200 x 65 x 50 cm
p 38

Untilted (2003)
Spirit level, model lorry wheels
6 x 100 x 2 cm
p 39

Decalogue (2001)
Skittles, enamel, vinyl lettering
Dimensions variable, 35 cm high
p 41

The Kingdom, or Evolution (2001)
Collaged paper on board
122 x 213 cm
pp 42–43

Key (to The Kingdom, or Evolution)
(2001)
Digital print on board
122 x 213 cm
pp 44–45 and inside cover

Castle Park (2000)
Wood, paint, table-tennis bats, nets
70 x 277 x 150 cm
p 47

Fresh Air (1998–2000)
Wood, paint, table-tennis bats, nets
Hyde Park: 70 x 287 x 140 cm
Regent's Park: 70 x 211 x 204 cm
Battersea Park (not pictured):
70 x 160 x 80 cm
pp 48–49

Break (2000)
Digital video
duration 17 mins
p 51

Augury (2000)
C Type prints (series of 5)
27 x 39 cm
p 52

Assembly (2000)
Lectern, projector, VHS on continuous loop
image size 40 x 50 cm, 136 cm high
p 53

No Evil Star (2002)
Digital video on DVD
duration 8 mins
soundtrack by Andy Moor
pp 54, 55

Marion Coutts

Born in 1964

1982–86
Edinburgh College of Art (BA Fine Art)

1989–90
Wroclaw School of Art, Wroclaw, Poland

Lives and works in London

Selected one-person exhibitions

2003
Kettle's Yard, Cambridge
Everglade, firstsite, Colchester;
Angel Row Gallery, Nottingham

2002
Cult, Chisenhale Gallery, London
No Evil Star, Hancock Museum,
Newcastle

2001
Palace, Aspex Gallery, Portsmouth
Bluecoat Gallery, Liverpool

2000
Yorkshire Sculpture Park

1998
RIBA Architecture Centre, London
Fresh Air, The Commercial Gallery,
London

1995
Project Gallery, Dublin
Galerie Clark, Montréal

Selected group exhibitions

2003
The Human Zoo, Hatton Gallery, Newcastle

2002
Fair Play, Angel Row Gallery, Nottingham
Games People Play, Storey Gallery,
Lancaster

2001
Fair Play, Danielle Arnaud, London
Cinematexas, Short Film Festival, Austin
*Images Festival of Independent Film and
Video*, Area Gallery, Toronto
Vito Acconci/Troubleshooting, Arnolfini,
Bristol
Broadcast, Clissold Park, London

2000
Viatico, Galerie Ek, Frankfurt
Dodorama, Rotterdam
Laboratory, firstsite, Colchester
New Work, Mappin Art Gallery, Sheffield
Without Day, City Art Centre, Edinburgh

1999
tongue 'n groove, VANE 99, Gateshead
Mostra, The British School at Rome
Marion Coutts/Pat Naldi, Cittá della
Scienza, Naples
Big Warm Open, Cambridge Darkroom

1998
Urban Paradise, The Changing Room,
Stirling
Marion Coutts/Emma Hathaway, Gasworks,
London
Smalls, Upstairs at the Clerk's House,
London

Awards and scholarships

2003–04
Kettle's Yard Fellowship, Cambridge

2000–01
Momart Fellowship, Tate Liverpool

2001
Woo Foundation Award

2000
London Arts Board Award

1999
Rome Scholarship, British School at Rome

1995
*British Council Montréal Professional
Exchange Grant*

1993–94
The Pollock-Krasner Foundation Award

1989–90
British Council Scholarship, Wroclaw
School of Art

Work in private collections and the
collection of Arts Council England

1986–94
Musician and performer with Dog Faced
Hermans; based in Amsterdam 1990–94,
touring throughout Europe, the US and
Canada

Selected publications

2003
Audio Arts, Volume 21, no 2, interview
with William Furlong
The Human Zoo, Hatton Gallery,
Newcastle, text by Steve Baker

2001
No Evil Star, Locus+, CD rom
Fair Play, Danielle Arnaud, text by
David Barrett
IF, Images Festival of Independent Film
and Video, Toronto
Vito Acconci/Troubleshooting, Arnolfini,
text by Catsou Roberts

2000
Without Day, Pocketbooks, text by
David Hopkins, edited by Alec Finlay
Marion Coutts, Yorkshire Sculpture
Park, text by Tom Lubbock

1999
Fine Arts 1998–1999, The British
School at Rome, text by Patrizia Mania

Selected articles and reviews

2003
Marion Coutts, James Hall, 'Artforum',
XLI – no 5, Jan, p 149
Club of Chaos, Dan Warburton,
'The Wire', issue 232, June, pp 30–34
Everglade, Amber Cowan, 'The Times',
7 June
Marion Coutts: firstsite, Robert Clark,
'The Guardian', 14 June

2002
Cult, Sally O'Reilly, 'Modern Painters',
vol 15, no 4, pp 138–139
Marion Coutts, interview with Carmen
Zita, 'TRACE', issue 1, Sept, pp 48–49
Cult, Elisabeth Mahoney, 'The Guardian',
5 Sept, p 22
B.Open, Laura Cumming, 'The Observer
Review', 14 July, p 11
Art Preview, Hannah Schuckburgh,
'Art Review', Sept
Cat's Eyes, Morgan Falconer, 'What's On',
4 Sept

2001
Welcome to my World, Vanessa Thorpe,
'The Observer Review', 30 Dec, p 8
Palace, Amber Cowan, 'The Times',
3 Nov
Animal rights and wrongs, Steve Baker,
'TATE' magazine, issue 26, pp 42–47
Playing Skittles in God's Alley, Stephen
Mitchell, 'Evening Standard', 1 Oct, p 54

Wide Impact, Dierdre Hanna, 'Now
Magazine', Toronto, 12 June
Marion Coutts, Jessica Lack, 'The
Guardian', 17 Nov
Profile, Ronnie Simpson, 'Art Review',
April, p 61
Marion Coutts, Vincent Deary, 'CVA',
issue 34, p 69
Animal Magic, Jenny Turner, 'The
Independent Magazine', 14 April,
pp 28–29
Artist Story, Marion Coutts, 'Artists'
Newsletter', Feb, p 66

2000
A Sound Way to Explore Sculpture,
Malcolm Handley, 'Liverpool Daily Post',
11 Oct
*Marion Coutts: Yorkshire Sculpture
Park*, Karen Wright, 'Modern Painters',
Autumn, p 117
Ballpark Figures, Maggie O'Farrell,
'The Independent on Sunday', 17 Sept,
pp 24–25
Marion Coutts: Yorkshire Sculpture Park,
Robert Clark, 'The Guardian', 9 Sept

1999
Thin on the Ground, Jennifer Higgie,
'Make', Dec 98–Feb 99
Artisti Inglesi a Napoli, 'Roma', 17 June
Video di Coutts e Naldi a Coroglio,
'Corriere della Sera', 25 May

Marion Coutts

Published by Film and Video Umbrella, in association with firstsite
Published in an edition of 1,000
ISBN: 190427005 0
Publication supported by the National Touring Programme of Arts Council England, with additional support from firstsite and from Goldsmiths' College, London

Edited by Steven Bode
Designed by Herman Lelie
Printed by PJ Printers, London

© Film and Video Umbrella, firstsite, the artist and the authors

Photo credits:
Douglas Atfield: 6–7, 16, 17, 23, 25, 32–33, 47, 53, 58–59; Marion Coutts: 18, 26–27, 51, 52, 54–55;
Alan Dimmick: inside back cover; Michael Doherty: 19; Robert Hind: cover, 8, 37, 39; John Lawrence: 14;
Roger Sinek: inside cover, 11, 12–13, 21, 38, 41, 42-43, 44–45; Edward Webb: 48–49

Other image credits: Thomas Bewick woodcuts: pp 28, 30; '1800 Woodcuts by Thomas Bewick and his School',
Dover Publications (1962); G.Kirkham (after Charlotte Reihlen), 'The Broad and Narrow Way' (1883): p 29;
Lithograph 57 x 47.5, British Museum 1999-4-25-13. © The British Museum, London

With thanks to the British Museum for permission to reproduce the 'Broad and the Narrow Way'.

Marion Coutts would like to thank:
Vincent Deary; Sally O'Reilly; Steven Bode, Mike Jones, Bevis Bowden and everyone at Film and Video Umbrella;
Katherine Wood, Annabel Longbourne and everyone at firstsite; Ed Salkeld; Locus+; Victoria Pomery; John Gill
and everyone at Chisenhale Gallery, London; Jo Bushnell at Aspex Gallery; Tate Liverpool; Catsou Roberts; Andy
Moor; Heather Deedman; Alec Finlay; Kathy Kenny; Herman Lelie and Stefania Bonelli

Special thanks to Tom Lubbock

Film and Video Umbrella
52 Bermondsey Street
London SE1 3UD
Tel 020 7407 7755   Fax 020 7407 7766
www.fvumbrella.com

firstsite
The Minories Art Gallery
74 High Street
Colchester CO1 1UE
Tel 01206 577 067   Fax 01206 577 161
www.firstsite.uk.net

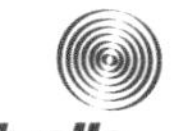
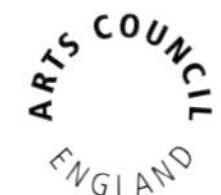
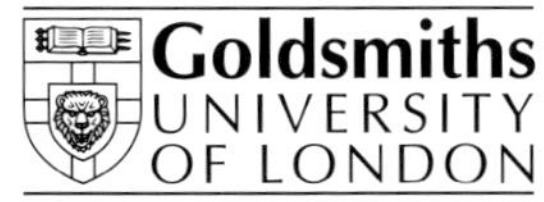